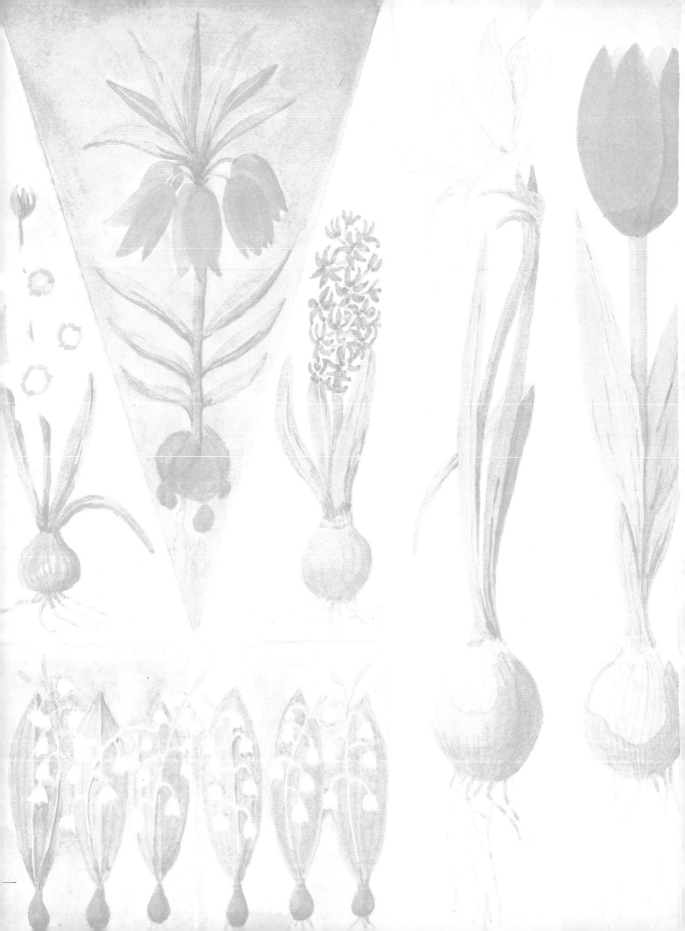

the STORY GARDEN

Cultivating Plants to Nurture Memories

the STORY GARDEN

Cultivating Plants to Nurture Memories

Ellen Sheppard Buchert & Johanna Buchert Smith

GIBBS SMITH
TO ENRICH AND INSPIRE HUMANKIND

First Edition

17 18 19 20 21   5 4 3 2 1

Published by
Gibbs Smith
P.O. Box 667
Layton, Utah 84041

1.800.835.4993 orders
www.gibbs-smith.com

Designed by Mina Bach
Authors'portraits on pages 8 and 15 painted by Amy Buchert
Printed and bound in Hong Kong

Gibbs Smith books are printed on either recycled, 100% post-consumer waste, FSC-certified papers or on paper
produced from sustainable PEFC-certified forest/controlled wood source. Learn more at www.pefc.org.

Library of Congress Cataloging-in-Publication Data
Names: Buchert, Ellen Sheppard, author, illustrator. | Buchert Smith, Johanna, author.
Title: The story garden : Cultivating plants to nurture memories / Ellen Sheppard
Buchert and Johanna Buchert Smith ; illustrations by Ellen Sheppard Buchert.
Description: First edition. | Layton, Utah : Gibbs Smith, 2017.
Identifiers: LCCN 2016031627 | ISBN 9781423645818 (jacketless hardcover)
Subjects: LCSH: Gardening.
Classification: LCC SB450.97 .B82 2017 | DDC 635--dc23
LC record available at https://lccn.loc.gov/2016031627

From Ellen

A sunflower to Rob for help with transportation, and a beautiful bower of chickpeas and lentils to Georgia, who fed us all. A giving pink grapefruit tree to Chris for doing some drives and babysitting, and to Amy for painting our portraits. Rabbitbrush for Marilyn Hayes and roses for Sue Parkinson for letting me use their studios and critiquing my paintings. Persimmons and apricots to Heather Jenkins, who babysat at a critical moment. A manzanita for John Muir Laws for his great YouTube tutorials on drawing birds and bugs. Fragrant French lilac for Jeanne for a tutorial on symbols, and for months of general cheering and support. An apple tree, a long-term commitment with roots that run deep, for George. His love, knowledge, advice, and patience have made this book possible.

From Johanna

A mountain lupine for Marlena Korpela, for doing all the canyon driving for childcare swaps, for her enthusiasm, and her instructive example of making working from home work; a yellow raspberry bush for Jodi from Montessori Children's Garden for creating a sunny, loving place my three-year-old loves to be; a bouquet of cosmos for Bethany Brady Spalding, a master craftswoman at seeing and articulating goodness and strength and imbuing confidence, and also for reading early drafts and letting me store plants in her fridge; a wild blue indigo for McArthur for enthusiasm and help with marketing; a bush of basil for Leah Moses for watching my kids while I worked, cheerleading, and being willing to take on the impossible; a bouquet of coneflower and black-eyed Susan for Jacqui Taylor, the estate of Eric Sloane, the estate of Robert Francis, and Patricia Lehnhardt, for permission to reprint their words. A blueberry bush for Rob, who spins a yarn finer than most and who allowed me to knit with it; an herb garden for Jeanne, auntie extraordinaire; and an orchard of rare and unusual fruits for our whole beloved family for their support and encouragement: thank you for letting us be part of your stories so yours and ours overlap. A blooming crabapple for Scout; a young dogwood for Finn, with loose bark for easy carving; and always a pie cherry tree for Eliot. In gratitude for windowsill real estate, a mature mango tree for my Andy.

And from us both

English lavender for Michelle Branson, our editor; the creative, capable team at Gibbs Smith; and our book's designer, Mina Bach. Thank you all. When you brush against a lavender bush as you walk by, its fragrance flows around each step you take. Like the scent of lavender, their contribution wafts through this work. For Suzanne Taylor, a sugar pine cone, full of seeds. As ever, thank you for the chance to grow.

CONTENTS

♡

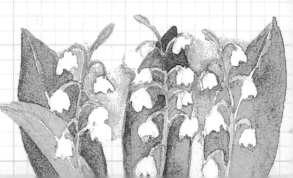

Helpful books and websites

Templates for activities given in the book

INTRODUCTION

Johanna

My earliest memory is
a botanical one: cross-country skiing with my family, finding some
wintergreen sticking out of the snow, snapping the shiny leaves in bits to
release the aromatic oils, and tasting the minty, mealy red berries. I was not
quite, or just barely, three. Because both my father's profession and my
mother's passion were botany related, it was natural that much of my growing-
up experiences connected me to plants. Family outings were to the arboretum
behind dad's lab; family picnics were to nearby undeveloped woods;
family chores included stacking firewood and working the garden;
childhood treats were dispensed upon memorization of botanical
Latin names. I thought we were just "unique," but one of the best
things about writing this book has been that once I've explained
its purpose to friends and acquaintances, almost universally
their faces light up as they immediately recall a beloved
person, place, or time whose memory is distilled in a plant.
It's a pleasure and a privilege to hear the delightful intimacies
of their everyday lives. Turns out, connecting memories to
plants isn't as unique to my family as my childhood self
imagined.

Almost every person I've spoken to about this project wanted to share their own story about a special tree, a special flower, a special garden vegetable, and the way it had meaning for them and someone they loved. Even the one person I spoke to who *couldn't* come up with any plant connection between him and another person—minus good food—eventually landed on a memory of daily bike rides through the wheat-planted Palouse in Washington, which brought back the details of a beautiful season of his own life. It may take you a moment of considering, but there's a good chance *you* connect a beloved person, time, or place from your personal history to a plant that they loved, that shared their space, was always on the menu, or that was a defining part of their setting in your own memories.

As humans, we long for connection to each other, and we often mourn the irreversible passage of time. We hold onto both with photographs and videos to try and keep specific moments nearby. The plants you grow can be another way you hold onto these things. They can be touchstones of celebrations, joyful events, and people. In *The Story Garden*, we show you how your garden can be a multisensory journal of people, places, events, and the celebrations of your life. As a book that focuses on the experience of the gardener as well as the creation of plants for the garden, this is a book of stories about the magic of self-discovery, memory, and human connections transmitted through botany.

Our goal is to help you create a different mindset about gardening.

In much the same way that your home can be a designer showcase of furnishings with no connection to the folks living with them, or—probably more to the point for many of us—an unedited collection of the stuff that has come your way to which you also may have no soul connection, your garden can also be on the deliberate end or the random end of the spectrum. Instead, grow the plants that really mean something to you. Grow the plants that bring you to one of the happy places or times or relationships in your life. In this way, your garden will become as individual as you are.

But we don't just want you to be inspired, we want you to be equipped with the basics of making more plants from plants, and so the stories in each chapter are supplemented by simple plant propagation how-tos.

There is a tremendous sense of accomplishment that comes from propagating plants, and a sense of preciousness that comes from propagating plants that tell part of your life story. We created this book to inspire you to find the botanical connections in your own stories, and to give you the skills you need to propagate those plants in a spirit of can-do-ism. Is it exhaustive on the details of every plant you might encounter? No. That's what Wikipedia and YouTube are for. But it will teach you what you need to know to not be afraid to try (and succeed) with a wide variety of common plants that grow all over the United States and Canada. And it gives firsthand accounts of why preserving family heirloom botanicals matters, or how to cultivate new ones.

Each chapter includes:

Inspiration *Stories from our memories to help prompt your own and inspire you to know where to look in your own life story.*

Skill instruction *A how-to guide to the basics of ten different simple, doable propagation techniques.*

Guidance *Most plants can be propagated by more than one method, so how do you know which method to use? For each propagation technique, we give you easy guidelines to help you decide.*

A plant list *Some other common plants for which this technique will work.*

Projects and, well, tangents *Interesting facts, recipes, gifts to make, and other ways to use the plants you've propagated.*

Want an especially easy project to get your feet wet with this concept? Turn to Water Rooting, page 17, and try pussy willows, geranium, or mint. Find your plant material needing to travel a bit? Turn to Leaf Cuttings, page 53; it's possible your intended plants might be able to grow from a leaf or two tucked into a ziplock, mailed in an envelope from point A and propagated on a windowsill at point B. Interested in including a packet of seeds from Great-Aunt Rita's place on Lake Michigan, along with a cool photo of Chicago you're gifting someone dear to you? Turn to Simple Seed Saving, page 105, to learn how easy it is to save seeds from flowering perennials you love, and for the link to a free printable seed envelope we made for you to keep it simple. In Planting Pups, page 39, you'll find a blueprint for a baby shower that includes a sweet and silly planting activity.

It's a great example of how including botanicals as a thoughtful part of your celebrations can transform them into vibrant symbols for your friends and family so they're no longer just about something from *your* past. They are the start of a happy memory association for those you love, too. Turn to Root Division, page 83, to learn how to dig and divide; in a time when it is not unusual to move long distances around the country, the work of reestablishing home can be shortened by knowing how to carry your significant plants with you.

So, who is this book for?

If you're a novice gardener who has never considered growing your own plants and have no idea how to do it, it's for you.

If you're an experienced gardener looking to be inspired by others' experiences and broaden your motivation for propagating plants, it's for you.

If you are someone who would love a peek into the cross section of plants and memories of other gardeners and creative types, it's for you.

If you are somebody interested in the homemade and homegrown, simple and inexpensive ways to promote happiness, connection over consumption, modern homemaking, journaling, doing something meaningful for free, or giving handmade gifts—we're pretty certain there's something here you'll enjoy, identify with, learn from, or be inspired by.

Finally, we want you to know these are techniques we use ourselves in propagating many kinds of plants, all toward the goal of living a more delicious, beautiful, conscious, deeply connected life. Obviously, we believe in the power of plants. But just as much, we believe in the power of stories—the ones we tell ourselves, the ones we tell to others, the ones we hear from others. We know from experience how a bush, a tree, a flower, a shrub, a grass—a living, breathing plant—can be the token that brings the story back, the symbol that keeps it alive, the link that keeps you connected, and the living root for future stories to grow from. In the chapters that follow, you'll find our stories. But what are your stories?

A note about the storytelling

Throughout this book, you'll read stories in two different voices: Ellen's (my mum) and Johanna's (mine). We hope you enjoy hearing about creating a memory garden from the different perspectives.

Start a rosebush from the sweet, old-fashioned bush in the family cemetery. As you walk out your kitchen door, enjoy brushing past a patch of the exact same mint your aunt Margaret used to make a sauce for the Easter lamb each spring. Tucked in a back corner of the yard is Grandma's hollyhock that grew beside her clothesline at the farm (you can almost smell the sun-dried sheets each time you look that way), and beside it, the catmint from the garden of the great dentist who made things better. Lemon verbena brings sweet memories of the first year of marriage, the first garden. The sweet Walla Walla onions in the vegetable garden are directly descended from an onion gift the generous host of a B&B in Washington placed in your hand as you left the house; vacation-relaxation warms your onion bed with memories of that happy family trip. The sedum that grows so independently across the front garden is the same sedum that grows in the yard of your favorite professor, ready to spring your memory back to your college years. The fig tree growing in the protected corner by your garage is a reminder of sweet summer walks on that same campus, while the balsam fir at the end of the driveway is pure Christmas.

So go snip, split, separate, submerge, plunder, plant, gather and harvest, dig and divide. Enjoy the process of making more plants, and enjoy the harvest: a garden of your life's tales.

Ellen

I grew up in a little town of eight hundred people surrounded by farms—dairy farms, peach and apple orchards, hay fields. We grew hollyhocks and lima beans in the backyard, and my dad's best friend was the county agent who taught me that plants had Latin names and lives of their own. I've been around awhile—I remember seeing pictures in *Life* magazine of old Civil War veterans marching in Memorial Day parades—but plants have been an intrinsic part of my life since I was little. Grandpappy would recount stories about growing up on a farm in "South Jersey," retelling the taste of fresh tomatoes, sweet, sun-warmed cantaloupe, and the antics of his eight siblings. He, with the help of his mules, delivered milk from home-pastured, hand-milked cows to earn college tuition. One of my grandmas grew up on a tobacco farm in Connecticut, and my mother-in-law grew up on a farm commune near New York City. It was she who taught me to love basil and bay leaf and dill. I love plants and the warm memories I have associated with them.

A word about plant names: some plants have "common" or folk names (e.g., angel's trumpet, or, in Latin, *Brugmansia*), others don't (e.g., *Caladium*). Some have multiple common names (e.g., prairie rose-gentian, Texas star, meadow pink), and sometimes several different plants end up with the same common name (such as hens and chicks, see page 59). This can be confusing, and it's why oftentimes books about plants will strictly use Latin names to refer to each plant—as a way to avoid ambiguity. But because one of our goals in writing this book is to make plant propagating accessible and commonplace, we have chosen to use the common name when we can, clarify when we need to, and use the Latin botanical name as a last resort.

AMB

FARMALL

WATER ROOTING

WATER ROOTING

Aunt Turrie's Yard

ELLEN

It begins with a casually picked stem from a downtown garden bed, a pretty coleus, and memories of Turrie's whole yard come rushing back: the winter aconites in the shadow of Turrie's shed; the cold frames made of two-by-sixes topped with an old glazed window for starting the seeds early; the dinner plate dahlias.

Every year, she won the prize for the biggest dahlias in the county at the Flemington Fair. Those dahlias were way bigger than I was, and grew each year in the rectangular raised beds that took up most of Turrie's backyard. A path of flagstone ran from the back door of the house, west between the two long beds, to the small gray shed that occupied the site of the old outhouse, which had been before my time.

A sandwich plate–size box turtle shared the backyard with us in the summer, and since Turrie's backyard was separated from ours by just the packed-earth driveway, his escape route crossed it when he tired of children putting him into a cardboard box to "take care of him." He walked away to Turrie's to eat lettuces. "He is all right," our mother would explain. "He carries his house with him. When he wants to go to bed, he just pulls in his legs and head, and shuts the door." It sounded like camping to me; I loved camping.

Keturrah had never married. She lived with her parents and then without them, and by the time I was a little girl, she was an old lady. She took in boarders. One was Mr. C., who was the postmaster and ran the general store. He had been a school

18

principal when he was younger, and he liked children. He always carried candy in his pockets. We neighbor kids would run to him when he came home from work, to see what treat he had for us that night. But neither he, nor the other boarders, ever worked in the garden. That was all Turrie's.

Every year in the late summer, a magical, almost faerie-like event occurred in the garden. Tiny feathery Christmas trees appeared there, already decorated with red and green balls attached by the most delicate of threads. I loved them, and ran to show the wonder of them to Mother, who thought they were beautiful too. Decades passed before I learned they were female asparagus stalks gone to seed.

Turrie's coleus plants grew in long boxes on each side of her shady flagstone front walk, and while all the other leaves I knew were green, the colors of these encompassed half the rainbow. The bright plants almost fluoresced with yellow, red, and purple, and their leaf edges ruffled with orange or chartreuse. What a wonder! No two leaves were alike. I know this because I looked and looked at them.

Every fall, Turrie somehow preserved them to set out again the following spring. She and I never discussed plant propagation, but this is what I think she did: she would have cut nonflowering stems that had not gone woody, and put them in a glass of water. Coleus plants are in the mint family. You can tell by the square stems. Members of the mint family all have square stems, and they all willingly grow pretty white roots in a glass of water.

Turrie would have likely made certain there were two or three leaf nodes on each stem, with the leaves removed below the water line. She would have changed the water every day until the roots grew, because it is only after the onset of roots that the water stays clear. Turrie would have kept the stems on a cool windowsill, out of direct sunlight, and enjoyed the delicate evidence of the life force within when the snow was flying without.

Then, when the days got longer, she would have potted and trimmed them to give the roots a chance to adjust to soil after all that easy water. She would, no doubt, enrich the soil in her planters with composted manure. By the time the robins sang their throbbing spring chorus in the Norway maples, the coleus would be ready to set out in their boxes.

New Sprigs from an Ancient Forest

JOHANNA

When our family made the trip to the north of California to see the last of the old-growth coastal redwoods and ragged ocean cliffs, I didn't expect it to feel like a pilgrimage, nor the walks so sacred. For our three young children, it was impossible to take walks without collecting the beautiful, tiny redwood cones, and the shells and agates on the beach. But despite our handfuls of treasures, it is the rosemary snips I have rooting in a glass on the windowsill that will be a cheerful reminder of the sweet little farmhouse on the coast where we spent eight happy days.

The robust and bushy rosemary plant that greeted us every time we stepped outside the front door became part of most meals we prepared. As I cook with my northern California rosemary over the next years, that rocky coast, those ancient trees, but mostly the sweet hours of uncomplicated time as a family, will be part of my enjoyment of the rosemary in my own yard, on my own cutting board, in my own spice cupboard.

Jeanne's Mint Salsa

My sister Jeanne is always happy to supply a sprig of mint for water rooting. The best thing she does with it, besides sharing, is make this. Based off a simple mint chutney recipe, this bright, delicious condiment should flexibly showcase whatever is ripe and in season alongside the basic ingredients.

> 1 CUP MINT LEAVES, TIGHTLY PACKED
>
> $1/2$ CUP CHOPPED ONION (OR LESS IF IT'S A STRONG, PEPPERY ONION)
>
> JUICE OF 1 LIME
>
> CHILE PEPPER, TO TASTE
>
> $1/2$ TEASPOON SUGAR, OR MORE TO TASTE

Blend this all up in the blender to a fine paste. Voilà.

Eat it with spicy Indian food and naan, or with "nut quesadillas"—toasty warm corn tortillas sandwiching cheese and chopped toasted nuts.

Because the salsa has a tendency to turn a funny brown color as the mint leaves oxidize, it's best if served within 15 minutes of being made. If you chop the leaves rather than blend them, they will stay green longer. Technically, the salsa will keep in an airtight container in the fridge for a week; you'll just have to get over the color. But it's so delish, that won't be difficult.

Jeanne's Magic

Get creative with substitutions for the mint leaves and the sugar. "Any herbal thing you can find, throw in little bits of it." There are countless yummy variations; here are a few of hers:

Spring: *To the basic ingredients, add (in combination, or alone) chopped violets, yarrow leaves, fennel leaves, sweet cicely, cilantro, parsley, or lovage. Switch out the sugar for finely chopped strawberries or apricots.*

Summer: *To the basic ingredients, add (in combination, or alone) chopped nasturtiums (blossoms or leaves), dill, rose petals, basil, or celery leaves. Switch out the sugar for fresh raspberries, blueberries, or finely chopped plums.*

Fall: *Add the same amount of apple as onion (this can be added in the blender, as puréeing it together won't turn the salsa an unpleasant color), or add some diced peach instead of the sugar.*

Winter: *Toss in a few handfuls of pomegranate seeds, jewel-like red amidst the green, to replace the sugar for an especially pretty mix of colors.*

Water Rooting

How

This most simple of propagating methods is partly as fun as it is because you can see all the action: pretty white water roots forming on your cutting. That said, water roots (roots that grow in water, as opposed to soil roots, which, you guessed it, grow in soil) can be brittle, tender. The most difficult part of the whole process is the last one (and it's not difficult, it just requires taking care), so pay attention to the last step.

ONE

At a clean angle, cut sprigs 4 to 6 inches from a growing tip, avoiding stems that are blooming. Dormant stems will be difficult or impossible to root.

TWO

Remove the leaves from the bottom half or so of the stem. There should be at least one leaf pair still on the stem.

THREE

Place the cuttings in a cup, jar, or container of some kind where at least the top third of the plant is above the rim. Fill the cup with water to just below where the leaves start; keep the leafless part of the stem underwater.

FOUR

Place it in a warm, bright spot out of direct sunlight. Windowsills are often ideal.

FIVE

Change the water every day to keep bacteria at bay.

SIX

When the roots are anywhere between $1/4$ and 1 inch long, you're ready to transplant. Some plants will achieve this in less than two weeks; others may take up to two months. As long as your cutting isn't rotting, don't give up. If it is rotting, definitely compost it and start over. Leaving the roots to grow into a tangle will reduce their chances of surviving transplanting to soil. At this point, you will basically be weaning your little starts off water.

Do not put them directly into outside soil; carefully transfer them to a pot and cover with prewetted soil. Now give them their own little plastic bag greenhouse and keep them moist. Gradually, say, over the course of two weeks, cut holes in the bag until the plants are exposed to air of the same humidity as outside the bag. Once they are established in pots and have switched gears from water roots to soil roots, they will be ready to harden off and transplant outdoors.

When

Spring, when everything is in vigorous growth, if you've got options and you're looking to make lots of new plants. End of summer, before the last frost, if you're looking to keep cuttings to replant next spring.

Why

When you're too busy to plant, this technique is a good way of holding cuttings until you can get to planting them in soil. At the end of summer, this method saves tender plants to use again the following spring. You can even use this method when you're simply interested in watching roots grow.

Glossary

harden off: The gradual process of getting a plant that is accustomed to a protected environment (like your home or greenhouse) adapted to outdoor conditions such as temperature variation, direct sun, and wind.

Who

There are many, some of which are: mint, geranium, lavender, basil, lemon verbena, chrysanthemum, lemongrass stalks from the market, sweet potato vine, coleus, oleander, euonymus, butterfly bush, trumpet flower bush (brugmansia), ivy, even tomato suckers. And sometimes rose, if you're lucky.

Difficulty

Easy.

STEM CUTTINGS

STEM CUTTINGS

Finding the Life Force in Rods and Sticks

ELLEN

I had a stick when I was eight. It was as tall as I was, straight, a good inch in diameter, but light with a pithy core—perhaps sumac. Sumac branches can be like that. It was dear to me, and I called it my "good stick."

I found it already cut and trimmed in the woods behind my grandparent's house. The pith especially interested me. I carved rings in the thin bark, but the dry pith at each end especially interested me. I dug hollows in it by poking at it with a smaller twig.

Faeries often filled my thoughts at that age, and I saw them, almost, out of the corner of my eye. I knew they curled up in small spaces when they rested, like in the knotholes of Grandpappy's pear tree and maybe even in the soft hollows at the end of my stick.

Sticks were an accepted part of my family's culture. My mother whittled sticks into caged balls and letter openers. My dad and little brother made bows and arrows together. I carried my good stick around for years, tapping the damp rocks in the railroad culvert, the walls of Doc Miller's house, and wooden telephone poles that marched up our street. I carried it for walks at Valley Forge and Ken Lockwood Gorge, and on camping trips to High Point State Park. When I went to bed, I put it away in the corner of my closet beside the warm brick chimney that towered up three stories from the coal furnace in the cellar.

My good stick never flushed out, but I have always been captivated by the Old Testament story about Aaron's rod that bloomed. Like his brother Moses, Aaron carried a good stick. It was severed from its roots, but when it sprouted, bloomed, and bore ripe almonds, the people understood, unequivocally, God's

28

will. Pharaoh, Moses's nemesis, may have had his soldiers and chariots, but this miraculous fruiting was evidence to the children of Israel of a greater power, one that could control the life force of the earth and seasons, and bring a dead stick back to life. Other writings claim the rod bore sweet almonds on one side and bitter almonds on the other, and one or the other prevailed, depending on the behavior of the children of Israel; it acted as a visual guiding instrument, an obedience barometer.

Obedience aside, in some stems the life force is strong, and the species tends toward sprouting. Take the ancient crabapple tree in our backyard. Every year from unlikely places along the big branches and even from the trunk, it sends up water shoots (also known as water sprouts): tall, straight branches that reach, like the Tower of Babel, for the sky, and that grow at an amazing pace. But unlike Aaron's rod, this tree's roots run deep and far, and those water shoot rods are part of an intact, living tree.

Willows, however, really *want* to grow roots and shoots, attached to the tree or not—almost animatedly, like the willow in the forest that bordered the hobbits' Shire in Tolkien's Middle Earth. That willow wove malevolence only Tom Bombadil could control with his rhythmic song. The willows I know are tamer, beautiful and graceful, although their love of sun and water may tempt them to clog the drain line, or block up the septic system.

Willow *withies*, cuttings of young, flexible willow branches, have long been used to start living fences. You can simply stick the butt end of the shoot inches into the ground, making sure at least two to three leaf buds are above ground, spacing them about 9 inches apart, then angle more shoots, also pushed into the ground in each direction, and weave them together with a horizontal bundle of branches several feet off the ground. The first year, the shoots will develop roots and leaves if they have plenty of water and sun. The next year, the willows will send out branches that need to be woven back into the structure. If you just cut them off, you chance awakening the many-headed dragon told of in tales recounting the daring and valor of princes and heroes. As the legend goes, a brave hero cut off a dragon's head with the sharp, tempered blade of his sword. To his regret and dismay, the dragon did not die, but quickly grew ten heads sprouting from the stump of its neck, each roaring mouth opening to show razor teeth and breath of flame. Willows tend to do that too; cutting stimulates the growth of multiple stems. So, if the branch is straight, weave it back into the fence. It will be less work in the end. (Of course, if you *want* the dragon, this is called *coppicing*, and it's one way to get more withies.)

You can use your basketry skills to weave and grow other structures with willow as well, such as tunnels, half shells to cozy around the back of a garden bench, or igloo-shaped play houses with a dance of sunlight between the branches and leaves that rustle in the wind.

There you have it: three stories about sticks, the first a bit of nostalgia, remembering a stick that was my companion and tool, with the life force clearly found within the child that held it in her hands and imagination. The second describes a rod of power, a demonstration of God's control over life. The third tells of living wood; of a type of stick with the ability to grow roots of its own, becoming an exact genetic copy of the plant that it came from. Whether you carry it, wield it, cut it back, or weave it, you can find a life force in a good stick.

The Intercontinental Travels of a Levantine Fig

JOHANNA

Something can be a secret because it is hidden, or something can be a secret because it is unseen. The campus fig tree was a secret partly because of the former; it *was* tucked behind the university greenhouses, between their warmth and the side of a hill, which sheltered it from cold and snowy winters. Mainly, though, its visibility was cloaked because of the latter; a paved footpath ran right beside it, but how many students know what a fresh fig tastes like, let alone the tree it grows on? However, some of us *did* know, and from then on, all the members of that society, unknown to each other, kept tabs on the growth of those squat-bottomed fruits as they ripened from pale green to a soft, brownish burgundy. Then, of course, the mission was to harvest what you could, without being seen, so as not to give away to any potential competitors that there was a gourmet edible, free for the taking, right there on campus.

The delicious flavor and the joy of the secrecy were two of the pleasures that fig tree offered. The third was the lore of its origin, which made the pilfering of its fruit more exciting: a slip of stem, cut from an ancient fig in the Middle East, tucked into the breast pocket of a botany professor, smuggled across the Atlantic and nearly all the way across North America, rooted, and then planted in plain sight where nobody would find it. I enjoyed the fourth pleasure secondhand: the ease with which fig trees will propagate from stem cuttings. And so although that part of campus was renovated—the greenhouses moved, the fig tree removed—it is remembered and perpetuated in the two lovely little trees that began as a slip of stem, poked into wet sand and given a personal plastic-bag greenhouse until they were rooted and planted in the protected south-facing courtyard of my sister-in-law's home. Because free, fresh figs are a holy grail for gleaners and planters.

Coppicing

To coppice is to cut a tree or shrub to ground level to encourage the bushy growth of many branches. Sometimes this is done to create a windbreak or a deer-proof hedge, sometimes as a way to "farm" withies for other uses, or to create biomass for fuel. In Sweden, Denmark, and other countries, farmers grow crops of willows in rows in fields. To propagate more willows, they harvest withies during winter dormancy and then plant them out in the spring. That first spring and summer, the stem cuttings root and send up one or two shoots, and the next season, they are ready to harvest and chip up for biofuel in local heating plants. The following year, the healthy stump and roots send up more shoots, and harvest continues on a two-year rotation.

cut back

Rootstocks

If you are taking a cutting from a grafted plant, then the stem cuttings you are propagating will not have all the same characteristics as the plant you cut them from. This is because grafted plants combine the desired qualities of two different plants. The one in the ground is called the rootstock. These are usually selected to give the grafted plant traits such as hardiness, mature tree size, vigor, or resistance to drought and various diseases. The upper part of the grafted plant (called the scion) is selected for other traits (e.g., the color of the flower or the flavor of the fruit).

Many commercially sold plants are grafted onto rootstocks, and if you're buying a rose or a fruit tree or a new variety of flowering anything, it's likely on a rootstock. You can still propagate cuttings, just be aware that your new plant will not behave in identical ways to its parent plant. (That said, now that you're getting the hang of propagating, why not try your hand at grafting? It's very much within the realm of the possible for the everyday gardener.)

Willow Water
DIY "Rooting Hormone"

What makes willow so eager to grow from just a stem? Its chemistry. Auxins, or growth hormones, direct cell activity in plants. Two auxins are important in rooting: salicylic acid, which helps the cutting resist being overwhelmed by pathogens, and indolebutyric acid, which stimulates root growth. Both of these growth hormones are present in every variety of willow. Some people find willow water works well on its own; others find that the combination of willow water with a commercial rooting hormone is a more effective strategy than either one alone. We tend to like things DIY and organic (and free), so we're likely to use willow water on its own and take our chances most of the time.

To make willow water, gather about 2 cups of pencil-thin willow stems, clipped into 1- to 3-inch pieces. Make sure the leaves are removed; tips of stems may be the most potent. Pour 8 cups boiling water over the willow and let steep for at least 24 hours. An alternative technique is the sun tea method, where you cover the clipped willow stems with unheated water, and then let sit in the sunshine for at least 2 or 3 days. At this point, you can strain out the stems and refrigerate the water in a jar with an airtight lid for up to 2 months; after that it starts losing potency. Filtering and storing is the same for both methods.

There are several ways to use willow water. You can soak the stem cutting you are trying to root in the water overnight before planting it. You can use willow water for water rooting (see page 17). You can use it to water seeds or little seedlings already planted in soil. (Two applications should be sufficient.)

How

These general principles apply to many, many plants, but to be certain, look up the plant you're planning to work on for species-specific details. Remember to keep the cuttings damp the entire time you're working with them and out of direct sunlight until they are nicely rooted. Finally, don't forget to label your cuttings! Especially if you're doing more than one kind of plant, it can be easy to forget what is what, from where, or from whom while they are all in the little-sticks-in-pots phase.

ONE

Select the right stem to cut, making sure to cut below a leaf node, exposing the meristem. (Do more than one. Do a bunch; the chances of you getting one that takes are higher the more you do.) You want about 6 inches of a strong, healthy stem from this or last season's growth.

TWO

Remove the lower leaves.

THREE

Optional: Dip the cut end into rooting hormone (or willow water, see page 33).

FOUR

Get your pot ready, and put your cutting in. To get it ready, thoroughly wet the soil before you insert the cutting. *Many different soils will work as long as they allow good drainage (if not, the cutting will rot) and have some aeration (i.e., they aren't all compacted and dense). Make it easy for the little roots to push through.*

FIVE

Cover the cutting to keep it hydrated. You can do this by covering the cutting with a plastic bag, commercial propagator, clear plastic bottle (whose bottom has been cut off and whose lid is still on), or even an old-fashioned glass garden cloche. The point is to keep water vapor around your little cutting, since for the moment, it doesn't have its own roots to suck up water. Put it in a bright spot out of direct sunlight.

SIX

Wait for the strike! Different plants take different lengths of time to produce roots, and different growing conditions will affect this too. As long as your cutting looks alive (not dried up, not moldy), don't give up.

You'll know your little starts have rooted when they begin showing new growth. You can then gradually wean them from their greenhouses and harden them off, but they will often benefit from developing bigger root systems in pots before they are ready to go in the ground outside.

When

Softwood cuttings (new growth that is almost fully developed) taken in the early spring have the best chance of rooting but are in most need of a humid growing environment. Hardwood cuttings (fully hardened-off plant material from the current year) are best taken in the late fall and through the winter months, or while the plant is dormant.

Why

You may use this method when you want a whole lot of clones; perhaps you will be giving a plant start to everyone in your book group, or one to each of the nieces and nephews, or if you want to start an espalier project, windbreak, or hedge. Or you may want to preserve a known variety; you want Grandma's apricot tree, not the potential varieties that would come from its seed.

Who

Bittersweet, blackberry, boxwood, Chinese hibiscus, clematis, cotoneaster, dogwood, elderberry, English ivy, evergreen azalea, flowering quince, grape, holly, honeysuckle, hydrangea, lilac, magnolia, rhododendron, rose, spirea, viburnum, willow, and many more.

Difficulty

Easy to moderately difficult, depending on the species and whether you are rooting hardwood or softwood cuttings.

Glossary

leaf node: The small swelling on a branch where a leaf, or leaves, grow out.

meristem: Undifferentiated cells found in parts of plants where growth can take place; can become any type of plant tissue, much like stem cells in animals.

strike: To grow roots. For example, hardwood (cuttings taken at the end of summer or when the plant is dormant) will generally take longer to strike than softwood (cuttings taken in the spring), which is eager to strike since it is full of growth hormone.

rootstock: The root of a grafted tree or bush. If a shoot grows from the rootstock, it will bear genetically different flowers and fruit from the scion.

scion: A branch or a bud, grafted to a rootstock to give a plant desirable qualities of fruit or flower.

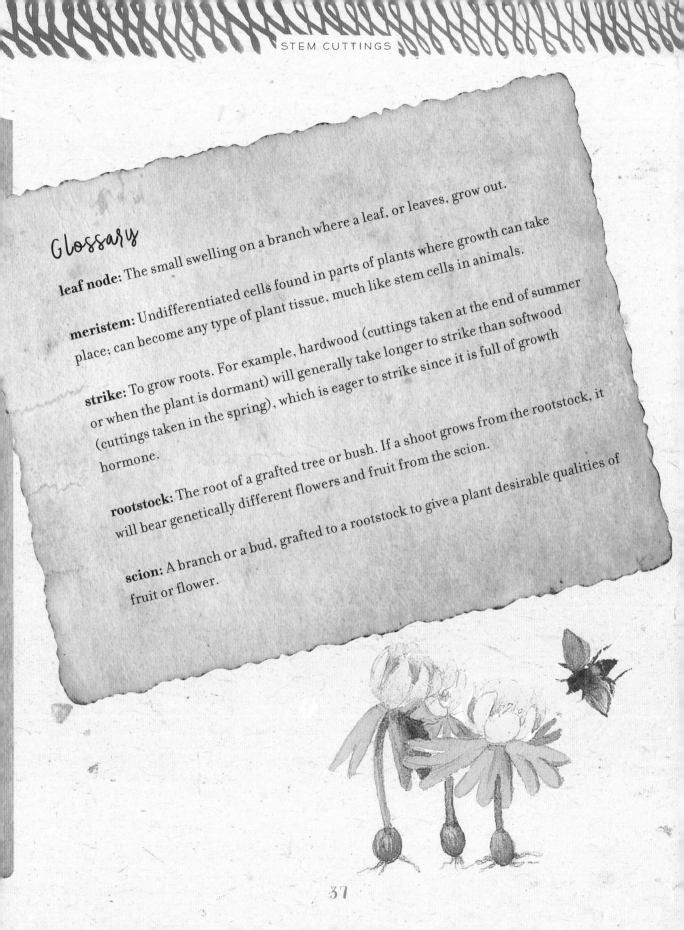

PLANTING
PUPS

PLANTING PUPS

Aloe by the Book

JOHANNA

As a child in Toronto, aloe was a plant that sat in a hard water–crusted pot on the windowsill, all chubby, curving stems, prickly on the edges, healed with a dry seam at the broken-off tips. It was the automatic second place to turn after a burn (ice first), and since my family has had a preoccupation with fire as long as I can remember—an old-fashioned wood stove in the living room that necessitated removing the ashes, possibly the coals, as part of our regular chores; camp fires for cookouts in the arboretum behind dad's lab for special times; and later, giant brush fires, 6 feet by 12 feet, as we cleared land for a home and road further north—it had tips broken off regularly. I never saw an aloe with sharp-tipped leaves as a child.

As an adult, I moved for a season with my own little children, ages one and three, to Malawi, a small, landlocked country in southeast Africa. It wasn't until we took a trip south to a managed forest during the dry season that I saw aloe growing in the wild, to its full potential. You'd expect Malawi to be tropically hot—it's considered an equatorial climate—but in the mountains, this is tempered, and in the dry season, nighttime temperatures can swing to near freezing. After being in the capital city for a year, it was like putting aloe on a burn to get out into woods and put a canoe in the water. The lodge had a big cozy fireplace; we read bedtime stories there, a few favorites we carried around with us—an illustrated excerpt from *The Song of Hiawatha,* and a book of children's poetry from South Africa—and then stepped outside to walk to our cabin. The cold night air was only part of what made us draw in our breath. Above us, frosty clear, was the most amazing field of darkness crowded with stars, and the children saw for themselves "the broad white road in heaven." It was like having a view into ancient history, sharing something with all of humanity.

The next morning, it warmed up quickly—a bright clear day. We walked along the trail, through tall bushy grasses, and past prickly bushes, busy nubbly anthills, and gorgeous curving spikes of a plant that could have been invented by Dr. Seuss. It's long leaves sprang from the soil, curved slightly in thick bends around tall central spires covered in deep-orange florets that gradually changed to yellow at the stem end. They were as tall as my three-year-old daughter, who was delighted, once we identified them as aloes, to look them in the eye and introduce herself, reciting a favorite poem:

> *Hallo Aloe,*
>
> *How are you?*
>
> *Reaching up to sky of blue?*
>
> *It seems to me*
>
> *Your claims to fame*
>
> *Are leathery leaves*
>
> *And flowers of flame.*
>
> Jacqui Taylor, "A Baobab Is Big"

Bromeliad Pups

ELLEN

A science colleague of my husband George's, Al G., invited us to see his collection of Cree and Inuit art. Lovely things they were, and quite unlike the simple bears and seals done for tourists. There were intricate soapstone carvings, one of them a many-figured piece of the turtle-earth creation myth; delicate beadwork; and paintings with symbols and colors that drew from the wilderness of the North. Hours passed quickly listening to Al's stories, our eyes riveted to his bright blue ones that sparkled under a thick shock of white hair.

When the stories flagged a bit, Al asked if we would like to see his bromeliad collection. He took us to a tiled area at the foot of the staircase to his office loft. Surrounding the sides of the stairs were pots and pots, each with a bromeliad plant. They were lit by a skylight in the ceiling above and looked healthy and well cared for. Some were in bloom, their final burst of color before they fade and die—spikes of orange, red, purple, yellow. But they likely wouldn't die before growing pups close to their stems. Pups are not really babies, more like little immature clones of the "mother" plant. Al knew them all, excitedly telling us their names and their tropical country of origin.

"I'm really excited by bromeliads," he told us.

Excitement is contagious. And memorable. Here it is twenty years later, and while I was at the grocery store today, I noticed a cart full of marked-down bromeliads. I picked one up to really look at the bright-red bracts ascending the stem and check to see if it had started a pup. It had. No doubt they are from a greenhouse, and

42

not a country of origin, but a lot of memories bunched up to get to the surface all at once, and I think I just caught a flash from a pair of Newman-blue eyes.

Welcome a Little Bird: A Baby Shower Blueprint

How do you throw a shower for a fifty-year-old new-mom-to-be, and a twenty-one-year-old birth-mom-to-be? Ask a friend with a beautiful backyard garden to host, and follow these simple guidelines to welcome all the hens and the soon-to-arrive little chick. Because the mom-to-be had lived in the same community for so long and there was such a sense of joy and celebration and gratitude for her becoming a mother, there would be many people wanting to meet both mothers, show their love and encouragement, and express their joy at such a tender time. We made the shower an open house so people could come and go and introductions (and treat nibbling) could happen at any time. The activities chosen reflected the new mama's love of words, personal storytelling, and her offbeat sense of humor.

Activities

Something for the Mama

Have a table and chairs dedicated to this activity. Supply some beautiful origami paper and several sets of instructions on folding a simple paper crane (see page 142 for a template). Before they start folding, have the guests think of a special, powerful word for the new-mom-to-be (or babe), and write it on the inner side of the paper. (A few examples: chocolate, brave, sleep, dahlia, snuggles, courage, kindness, faith, miracle, strength, gratitude.) When they have finished writing and folding, the little paper talismans can be collected in a bowl or cylinder vase to send home to display as is, or to hang from threads in the nursery, a flock-like cloud of loving thoughts and wishes.

Something for the Little Bird

Create an intimate space for a story-and-lullaby recording booth using two benches or a few chairs around a card table, and draping curtains, lengths of fabric, or even tablecloths around them. When guests feel like there is privacy but the stakes are low, they will be more candid and less self-conscious. Provide some sample questions to get people thinking and talking. (See below for a few to get you started; we selected from several sets of "Table Topics" the most interesting, and shower-appropriate, questions.) Provide a high-quality audio recorder—a smartphone would work just fine, as long as the microphone is pointing at anyone who is doing the talking. People who are uncomfortable being interviewed may prefer to hum or sing a familiar or favorite lullaby. The audio record this will create can be made into a CD for baby to listen to, or could make fun listening for mama during the wakeful night hours that are just around the corner.

Here are a few interview questions to have on hand for a story-and-lullaby booth:

(For more ideas, see the websites listed in the Resources section, page 138)

Sing or hum a lullaby you love. Why does it have meaning for you?

What's a song you remember being sung to you when you were a child?

What is your first childhood memory?

What is something you got caught doing that you weren't supposed to do as a child?

Who cut your hair as a child, and how was it styled?

Tell about summer vacations when you were a child.

Describe your childhood home.

What was something you loved doing with your mom or your dad as a child?

What's some parenting advice you've found useful (or ignored)?

Something for the Guests

Plant a hens and chicks pup in oddball toy planters, creating a bit of "journal garden" for each guest to bring home. This takes a fair bit of work beforehand, so start on this a few weeks early. We planted a few in advance to use as examples on the table. It's helpful to have your own garden of hens and chicks to unearth for this project, but if you don't have that available, you can buy them in bulk (see the Resources section, page 138).

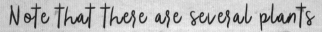

Note that there are several plants that go by the common name "hens and chicks," and they each need different conditions for growing. Check out page 59 to find out more.

Toy Planters

POTTING SOIL

A BIN OR BUCKET TO KEEP IT IN

50–60 HENS AND CHICKS PUPS, DUG UP BUT TUCKED IN SOIL TO KEEP THEIR ROSETTES CLEAN AND THEIR ROOTS HYDRATED

50–60 HOLLOW TOYS (ANIMALS WORK BEAUTIFULLY)

SPRAY PAINT TO THOROUGHLY COAT THE TOYS

AT THE SHOWER SITE, YOU WILL ALSO WANT ACCESS TO A HOSE FOR WATERING THE POTTED PLANTS AND FOR GUESTS TO RINSE THEIR HANDS IN.

ONE

Begin by visiting all the nearby secondhand stores and browsing through their toy sections. Because you will be using them as planters, the toys that will work best tend to be hollow, made out of a plastic that can be cut (you have to make a hole to put the soil in and that the pup will poke out of), and kind of "baby bear"-ish—not too big, not too small. Don't worry about colors; you will be spray-painting all of them.

TWO

Once you have enough (we gathered about 50, expecting that not all guests would be interested in doing a little gardening activity), cut a hole in the top, at least 2 inches in diameter if possible, where you will plant the pup.

THREE

Set the toys on a big piece of paper, and give them a nice coat of color. It's fun to see them transform from weird junk to sculptural beauties when they're all a shiny black, sunshine yellow, or bright cherry red. Don't rush this process. The different plastics take different lengths of time to dry and will take the paint in different ways. Be patient, give them several coats, and then flip them over and do the undersides. Once they've all dried, they are ready to be planters.

FOUR

At the party, set up a hens and chicks station. On a table that can get dirty and be rinsed, arrange the plants and the planters. Have the soil and water ready. Fill the toy planter with soil, and make a little hole to put the pup's stem in. Fill it in with soil and give it a good watering. Encourage guests to keep the soil moist but not wet, and keep in bright light.

Decorations

Pretty cloth tablecloths will go a long way to making an outside area feel festive. Don't feel like they have to match. Sometimes formality clashes with the goal of getting everybody to feel comfortable and open up creatively in the activities. A variety of vessels of flowers here and there are also instant beautifiers. We are big fans of using what is available nearby for bouquets. Stretch your flower budget and include some florist blooms among gleaned bouquets. Even twigs and branches or long grasses can be festive with bright paper flowers tucked here and there.

Place ornamental birdcages (see Resources section, page 138) around the party at varying heights; they could showcase pretty baby items, hold small bouquets, or just be empty.

Swooping garlands of any kind give a party a festive roof. Here, the garlands were strings of felt doves dyed in rich bright tones. (Look for the template on page 143.)

Soundtrack

You Are My Little Bird by Elizabeth Mitchell, from Smithsonian Folkways.

By turns mellow and peppy, this sweet little album of folk tunes sung in a woman's voice, with her husband and young daughter harmonizing, is just right for an afternoon party in a garden where there's lots of chatting, baby gifts, flowers, and some little kids running around. It's targeted to children, though entirely enjoyable for grownups, so it makes a nice little gift at the end of the shower too.

Refreshments

"Beautiful, delicious, and uncomplicated" are good guidelines when you're hosting an open-house shower outside. A cake, iced simply in white frosting but made elegant with various twigs, leaves, and flowers (rinsed and dried) from the garden, makes a dramatic focal point on the refreshments table. It can also be made in advance and iced the day of. Lemon bars are another tangy, sticky option, and they always look festive on the table. Mini quiches are fun thematically, can be purchased in bulk at Costco, and don't need to be kept warm to be yummy. Platters of fresh fruit (you can include a pretty-handled knife for slicing) make for colorful displays and delicious come-and-go snacking. Old-fashioned lollipops with wood sticks are what all the kids go for first. A drink dispenser with water and lemon is prettier than water bottles, and is simple, functional, and universally enjoyed.

Felt Dove Garland

WHITE FELT—ENOUGH TO CUT OUT AS MANY LITTLE BIRDS AS YOU'D LIKE (WOOL IS EXPENSIVE BUT WILL GIVE YOU BRIGHT COLORS; POLYESTER IS CHEAP BUT DOESN'T TAKE DYE AS WELL)

DIFFERENT COLORS OF FABRIC DYE

2 (18-INCH) PIECES OF GROSGRAIN RIBBON

SEWING MACHINE THREAD FOR SEW-STRINGING THEM TOGETHER

ONE

Trace the template onto a piece of something stiff—a cereal box from the recycling bin is great. Cut it out and use it to trace a bird on felt. Layer 2 or 3 pieces of felt together to cut a few out at once. Keep tracing and cutting until you have all the little birds you need to make the length you want.

TWO

Dye the felt pieces, following the instructions on the package. (Of course, you could use colored felt, but if you want color variation and nuance, try dyeing them yourself following the instructions on the box.)

THREE

Now that your felt birds are all cut, colored, and dried, it's time to sew them into a garland.

FOUR

Using a sewing machine, begin by sewing an 18-inch length of ribbon to the first bird. Make sure you attach it to the upper third of your cutout so it hangs the right direction. This will be one of your tying ends, so strengthen it by reverse stitching it. Clip your threads.

FIVE

Letting the machine run an inch of stitches between cutouts, begin feeding the cutouts through the sewing machine, always through the top third of the cutout. When you've reached the last cutout, clip your threads.

SIX

Sew the second piece of ribbon to the last bird in your garland in the same way you sewed the first.

SEVEN

Store your garland by either wrapping it around a book-size piece of cardboard, or by stacking the felt birds on top of each other in a layered pile and placing them in a ziplock bag, pressed airless so they can't move around. In this way, you'll avoid the headache of trying to untangle them when it's time to hang them again.

HOW

ONE

For soil-growing pups, prepare your pots. Most pup-producing plants need or prefer a light, well-draining soil, such as one made from perlite, bark, and potting soil. A mix of potting soil and sand is, for many plants, enough.

TWO

When the pup has grown to be at least one-third the size of the parent plant, it is ready to be detached and planted. With your hands, a pair of scissors, or pruners, separate the pup from the parent plant, snipping the runners or snapping off the pup. For air plants, gently twist downward at the base of the plant. Very few species require more strength than you can reasonably deliver with your fingers. If you're propagating an air plant, you're done!

THREE

Pop the pup in the soil up to the base of the leaves, and give it a good watering (although aloes like to sit in dry soil for a week). That's really it!

When

The longer pups are attached to their parent plant, the faster they will grow to maturity. However, in the case of bromeliads, the faster you remove pups, the more pups the parent plant is likely to produce before it dies. If a pup has its own roots, it's a good sign it's ready to pot up on its own, but often they don't and will still transplant just fine.

Why

For most of these plants, this is either the easiest or the only way to guarantee a viable reproduction, so it may just be your only option.

Who

Air plants, aloes, bromeliads, hens and chicks (including sempervivums, jovibarba, and echeveria), sago palms, and more.

Difficulty

Easy.

Glossary

bract: The leaflike structure usually found at the base of a plant's flower.

bromeliad: A family of tropical and subtropical plants related to pineapples. Many species grow on trees and take in water through air roots. The largest one, commonly called (in English) queen of the Andes, can grow to 10 feet, and produce a flower spike up to 32 feet tall. It only flowers and produces seeds about every forty years, and is considered an endangered species. The smallest bromeliad is Spanish moss. Air plants are bromeliads.

LEAF
CUTTINGS

LEAF CUTTINGS

Jade and Other Jewels

ELLEN

When my husband, George, returned from a work trip to Victoria, British Columbia, the first thing he said to me was, "You should see the jade tree in the Queen Victoria lobby!" He knew I loved jade trees because of my association with the one that once grew on my grandparents' glassed-in front porch. My brother, Robin, and I played out there each time we visited.

Grandmother kept a box of American Bricks (a popular building toy in the 1950s, and a precursor to Lego) out there, and her jade tree and collection of ruffly flowered, lavender-colored African violets. Grandpappy stored years' and years' worth of copies of *Reader's Digest* on the porch. Those magazines took up a whole wall, stacked from the floor to the bottom of the windows.

Robin built sturdy residential and railroad buildings on the porch floor with American Bricks, and I tastefully landscaped with jade leaves and African violet blossoms. When we got tired, we sat in the sun and read new jokes from the unending supply of *Reader's Digest*.

When Grandmother came out and saw her plants denuded, she never batted an eye. She actively listened to our enthusiastic explanation of our city planning project, and sincerely praised our creativity and the skillful execution of our ideas. She never once berated us for pulling her plants apart.

"Oh, those plants will grow new flowers," I heard her explain to my concerned mother. "And did you know," she added, "you can grow little jade trees and violet plants from their leaves?" She looked down at the thoughtfully placed leaves on the floor. "You just cover them with a little earth, and they grow." She made it sound easy. Almost planned. What's important, she implied, is the children, not the plants, and as she did that, she also reassured her daughter-in-law by seeing the good in her children. I hope God is giving her and Grandpappy sweet rewards for their empowering grandparenting.

I have a jade tree on my windowsill that grew from one of those leaves, and our African violet, a ruffly lavender-flowered one, blooms several times a year.

Kalanchoe: What's in a name?

There are about 125 species of this plant, and some of them have the most wonderful, descriptive common names: felt bush (perhaps belongs on a felt board?), donkey's ears, silver teaspoons, devil's backbone, cup kalanchoe (nicely alliterative), flapjacks, desert cabbage, mother of millions, and penwiper (personal favorite).

How

All the words in this section can make it seem complicated, but don't be fooled. This is a seriously easy way to make more plants, and when you see little roots coming or little baby plants sprouting from a leaf, it can seem like magic too. Just make sure you give them a nice, bright, indirect light, and keep them warm—around room temperature—for the first bit. They'll take longer to propagate in cooler temperatures. All these plants like to be grown in high humidity when possible, so start them out in a plastic bag tent or under a cloche, or whatever you can think of to keep the moist air in. After your new little plantlets appear, you're safe to remove the greenhouse incubators. That said, some are easier to grow than others, and with some you will plant the whole leaf, others just a cut part of a leaf. Here are the basics and a few details:

ONE

Select a healthy, full-grown but youngish leaf, and prepare a pot of well-draining soil. It needn't be particularly rich soil, but it can't be a water-heavy one. Wet soil will encourage rot, not growth, with these kinds of plants.

TWO

Whole leaf: For leaves with a petiole (African violet, peperomia, gloxinia), snap off a leaf including the petiole and insert the petiole into the pot of soil (or sand or perlite, etc.) that you got ready previously. Give it a good watering; in three to four weeks, you'll have roots coming from the base of the petiole. For leaves without a petiole (kalanchoe, echeveria, jade tree, and many other succulents), break off a whole leaf. Because these are all succulents, they need to be given time to dry out the break, or to callus, before being planted. We want them to root, not rot. Once they're nicely callused, stick them upright in the pot, about three-quarters down in the soil. Don't cover them all the way. Keep them in a nice warm spot with good indirect light, and keep the soil just slightly moist.

Cut leaf (streptocarpus, pineapple lily, or eucomis, sansevieria): Select a nearly mature leaf and remove it at the base from the parent plant. Using a clean, sharp knife, cut the leaf in half (smaller leaves) or into 2-inch strips (longer leaves) across the center vein. Insert the cut pieces into the soil, maintaining original up-and-down direction, about half or two-thirds of the way, firming up the soil around it.

THREE

Create a little greenhouse around the leaves you are propagating. A plastic bag propped up with skewers and tucked under the pot works, and so does a milk jug with the bottom cut off and the lid still on. Clear plastic clamshells that contained doughnuts or other baked treats are perfect. There are also all kinds of adorable little plastic or glass greenhouses just the right size to fit a pot or two or three if you want something decorative.

FOUR

Water each cutting and allow the water to drain. Keep the soil moist but not wet.

FIVE

When you see the little plantlets appear, you can take off the greenhouse. Let them get bigger, and then pot them up individually.

When

Ideally, in the growing season (usually spring to early summer), but many will propagate well any time.

Why

Because you're somewhere for a short time and want to grab a quick piece of the plant to bring home and propagate. If you knocked over a beloved jade tree and want to put together a lot of wonderful, inexpensive gifts. Your hens and chicks are getting leggy from winter's low light. Because you will be traveling with your bit of plant, especially if by plane.

Who

African violet, begonia, echeveria, gloxinia, jade tree (crassula), kalanchoe, peperomia, sansevieria (snake plant, mother-in-law's tongue), sedum, and more.

Difficulty

Pretty easy.

Glossary

petiole: The stalk between a leaf and plant stem; the stem of the leaf.

Know your leafy-ball plants

If you've fallen in love with succulents in the past few years, you may be excited by all the variety in these compact, architectural little beauties. But colors and leaf size aren't the only things that distinguish them. There are three main types of these leafy rosettes: sempervivum, jovibarba, and echeveria. All three poke out little "chicks," and may all go by the common names "hens and chicks" or "succulent." But if you're looking to propagate by leaf cutting, only one of them will work: echeveria. So how do you know which is which if you've been strolling through a rock garden with a dear friend, who just gave you wonderful news about her first pregnancy, and you want to keep that happy time alive for you both with a plant from that time and place? First, if you can snag a pup rather than just a leaf, do that because it will work for any of the three and you don't have to know which kind it is. Second, here are a couple characteristics that may help: echeveria leaves are chubby compared to semp leaves; semps bloom from the middle of the rosette, and when finished the whole plant dies, whereas echeveria can bloom season after season with no problem. Jovibarba can be chubby or lean in the leaf, but its little plantlets, or pups—or chicks!—detach easily and roll away, actually called "tumblers," whereas echeveria and sempervivum pups are firmly attached on runners. Finally, while both semps and jovibarbas are frost hardy, echeveria is not. For more details on how to propagate all three varieties, refer to the previous chapter, Planting Pups (page 39).

LAYERING

LAYERING

Knox's Hill

ELLEN

Knox's Hill is on the south side of the little New Jersey borough where I grew up. To reach the mound-shaped hill from my parents' house, you had to walk south of the center of town, across the railroad tracks, and on past the cheese factory, whose stinky effluent ran down the ditch by the side of the macadam-paved street. ("Mack-a-dam," my father pronounced it, so he could shock my mother with the "dam" part.)

The hill is one of those rounded remnants of the great and ancient Appalachian massif, worn away by eons of weather and glaciers. It is topped with a light, acidic, moist organic forest floor and tossed with stones and rocks, like raisins in Raisin Bran.

On the west side of the hill was a fairly steep-sloped hayfield where my parents, brother, and I sometimes took Sunday afternoon hikes. One sunny spring day with a strong breeze from the west, we puffed up to the top of the hayfield, where the forest tentatively sent out colonizing plants, like cedar and sumac, and Mother let my brother and me take our shirts off and run in the wind. I still remember the surprise I felt at the intensity of the sensation of the wind, the pleasure of its touch on my back and chest. We held our arms out, stretched our necks, and turned around and around, hair flying, laughing, embracing the wind.

The rest of the hill was forested. Not with huge old-growth trees; those had fallen to the crosscut saws of the Dutch and German settlers who came up the Delaware River in the 1700s, and traveled east until they found a place with water and wood and tillable soil. We could see remains of those fallen giants—rotted trunks and big root holes where a tree had been blown over in a hurricane. The third-growth oak, maple, and elm trees were tall nonetheless, and covered with rampant honeysuckle vines. The vines are happy to grow with their roots in tree shade and their intensely fragrant flowers in the dappled sunlight near the treetops. My brother and I, and a few years later, George, the boy I was falling deeply in love with, and I ran along the deer trails to find out where they took us, dug in root holes to hunt arrowheads, and swung on honeysuckle vines—like Tarzan, we thought. We knew the raucous call of the blue jay, the bark of the red fox, and the breath of the deer.

One afternoon, time sent us running home the shortest way—through the poison ivy above the old culvert, with its limestone stalactites. "Oh no," I said. "I get poison ivy pretty bad."

"I don't," said George, as he scooped me up in his arms and carried me all the way down Knox's Hill. I felt his heart beat against my side.

The last time I climbed Knox's Hill was the week my father died. Something about staying in the old house with Mother made me want to hike the deer trails, or at least see if they were still there. Dad's minister, Jill, said she'd like to go with me, so off we walked under the culvert, past the cheese factory and its smell, and its Osage oranges on the ground beside the road, past the poison ivy, and up the vine-tangled slope. The trails were still there, the fall leaves carpeted the ground, and—what was that? Shots rang through the air. I had not included deer season in my nostalgic plans. "This makes me a little nervous," Jill said. "I think we should do this fast."

"Okay," I said. We saw our breath in the crisp November air. Another shot rang out. We looked at each other and formed an additional plan: we added human-only noise to our speed, singing Christmas carols at the top of our voices.

Our plan worked. Nobody mistook us for deer, and the hike, after the long hospital vigil, did us both good.

Vines have an interesting way of making more vines: they grow new roots from stem segments that come in contact with the ground. This asexual reproduction is called layering. Here is how it happens naturally. A poison ivy or honeysuckle vine grows out across the ground seeking something to climb. As the days go by, litter falls to the forest floor and forms a new layer of duff, some of it on top of the vine stem. "Aha," thinks the honeysuckle. "I was above, but now I am beneath. I will grow roots." And it does.

Eventually, the roots grow long and full enough to nourish the new part of the vine climbing the next tree, and if something like a deer hoof should cut the connection to the parent plant, the new rooted shoot will be just fine. It will be a new plant.

Johanna, George, and I all saw another dynamic duo of natural layerers when we took shifts staying with Johanna's sister Heidi, and Todd, at their little place on Bainbridge Island, a ferry ride from Seattle, Washington. Usually energetic and creative, poor Heidi was sick in bed with her third pregnancy; Todd was at work on the mainland; and their toddler had taken to climbing on the electric stovetop and turning on the burners while she sat on them. Heavenly days! We knew they needed another pair of hands to help with the children, so we tag-teamed shifts, passing each other in the airport, privileged to help.

All over the island, in vacant lots and at the edges of wooded areas, were thickets of Scotch broom and blackberries, crowded together, reaching out with intense vitality for a spot to layer up another clone. It was January when I took my shift with the tired-out family and the new baby. The broom along the roads was beginning to bloom in the winter drizzle—here a spot of yellow, there another—like forsythia gone haywire. The blackberries (the children called them "bok blerries") were still dormant, waiting for sunshine. Overhead, crows flocked boisterously, figuring out who was building a nest with whom this year.

Someone once told me there were only three things worth writing about: birth, passionate love, and death. I am amazed to find that plant propagation by layering takes me back to all three!

64

Remembering Roses

JOHANNA

I wish, for your sake, you could know my dear friend Rosario. She's smart and funny, and as the daughter of an ingenious, passionate plant rescuer, she has seen just about every stage of growth of any edible plant. She also has the most amazing head of wavy black hair. We were out for a walk in our neighborhood, probably passing children back and forth between our houses, and passing a fragrant, blooming shrub of Austrian copper roses.

We could smell them before we saw them, and we paused to gather and finger some of the deeply hued shed petals off the ground. Coppers are naturally hardy and brilliant in their coloring. Their scent is as loud and wonderful as their color, and they've been around since at least the 1500s, as they feature in heraldic symbolism. They also grow on long, thin branches, which are easy to bend and layer. Unlike many newer rose varieties, the Austrian copper's single-petaled blooms last a day or so each, and the entire show is over in a week. But where each blossom lasted so briefly, there appears a beautiful, plump, red-orange rose hip.

"If only there were some way to wear, or eat, this color, this smell," I lamented.

"There is!" she said brightly. "Where I grew up in Chile, *rosa mosqueta* grow pink and wild; they're all over, so we make them into a jam and remember them all year."

Here is the recipe she gave me. Not only do I remember that ephemeral time of early summer when I eat it, but also my beautiful black-haired friend.

Rosa Mosqueta: Rose Hip Jelly

1 TO 2 POUNDS ROSE HIPS

SUGAR

In the fall, after a frost, gather the rose hips, a task most pleasant when you are wearing gloves and have a companion. A pound or two is enough to make a few small jars of jam. They should be soft but not squishy, an orangey-red but not orange or dark red. Wash them, split them, put them in a pot, and pour in enough water just to cover them.

Simmer for 15–20 minutes, until they break down a bit. Strain the juice through a sieve; press the rose hips to get all the pulp possible out of the preparation. Compost the seeds and skins left in the sieve. Measure the juicy pulp. Add the same amount of sugar. Bring back to a boil and simmer until it thickens. You'll know it's thick enough when you put a spoonful on a cool plate and a skin wrinkles across the top of it. Decant the jelly into the jars, clean the rims, put on lids, and keep in the fridge till it disappears.

Note: Adding crab apples or tart apples, such as Granny Smith, to the rose hips in the pulp-making stage will add natural pectin to the recipe, resulting in a more jelled jelly.

Make a Vine Wreath

Any long, twining plant stem will work for this; grape, wisteria, and even Virginia creeper or morning glory will fold and wind into beautiful circles. Just make sure, if you're using a very light vine like honeysuckle, to keep the size small.

ONE

Gather your vine pieces. Remove the leaves unless you are going to display them right away.

TWO

Begin forming a loop with the diameter you want for your finished wreath. Tiny vines make pretty napkin rings, and great big ones warm up the side of a barn, shed, compost bin, or chicken coop. And the sizes in between can be hung on a door or used for a table decoration, around a pillar candle, or as a crown for a fair maiden.

THREE

Hold the first loop, and make another to match it in the manner of coiling a rope. Wind the remainder of the vine around the loops, or braid it in and out of the loops to hold all the pieces together. Continue to add coils to your first loop, tucking the end of the vine between the loops and twists, until your wreath is as thick as you'd like it to be. Sometimes a little twine tied here and there to hold it together until it dries will be helpful.

FOUR

Let your vine dry flat for 1 week, or 2 weeks if it's a bendy one. Then you can remove the twine and decorate.

How

To propagate by layering is to confuse an aerial stem to grow roots while it is still part of an existing plant, and then to cut the connection, like cutting an umbilical cord, so the newly rooted bit suddenly must become an independent, self-sustaining organism. Layering doesn't have to be done naturally, like it is on Knox's Hill or Bainbridge Island. You can do this on purpose to propagate plants of choice, most successfully in the spring and the fall. Shrubs with flexible branches near the ground, like rambler roses, forsythia, or snowberry, layer well.

ONE

Select a longish branch that is pencil-sized in diameter. It should either be dormant in spring or mature in late summer.

TWO

Prepare the soil where the stem will be buried by loosening it and adding compost or peat moss.

THREE

Remove all leaves from the part of the stem to be buried, and wound it with a knife just below a leaf node, cutting from the stem toward the tip.

FOUR

Prop this wound open with a toothpick and dust with rooting hormone if you've got some.

FIVE

Fasten the branch into the ground with a V-shaped stick, and cover it with two or three inches of soil then mulch. Some plants are eager enough to layer that just covering part of the stem with soil and holding it down with a brick will be sufficient.

SIX

Prop the uncovered leafy tip of the branch in an upright position. Over the next season, even several seasons, water to keep the area moist.

SEVEN

Once the roots are well established, the best time to transplant is early spring, or fall. Wait until then to separate the layer from the parent plant. With viney plants, such as wisteria, ivy, or clematis, one can root several plants from one long flexible branch. This is called serpentine layering.

Air layering, also instigated by wounding and treating with rooting hormone, is used on woody plants. Instead of covering the wounded stem with soil, the stem is covered with moist sphagnum moss then wrapped in plastic or foil to give the new roots a safe place to develop. Artist and author Eric Sloane told a wonderful layering story in his 1965 book *A Reverence for Wood*. He tells of a couple, Ruth and Benjamin Dean, who moved from Connecticut to Ohio in 1810. Two years before they journeyed, Ruth propagated her apple tree. She "bent a branch of the tree downward . . . and after slicing through the tender bark so that some day it might root, she . . . inserted the branch into and through a pot of earth. For two seasons she had nursed the 'layering pot,' keeping it wrapped with cloths and watering it daily, until roots had emerged from the cut portion within the pot."

After she separated her little tree start from the "parent plant," she buried the pot in the ground beneath her apple tree until they were ready to travel. Then she unearthed the pot. "'I shall take care of watering and shading it till we get to Ohio,' she said. 'If the tree lives, it will be worth all the trouble. It will be taking some of our old place with us. It was our favorite tree—it came from England and it can make another historic trip.'

'Very well,' Benjamin consented."

Ironically, but successfully, they traveled west seeking a better place for their family, carrying with them the layered clone of their seek-no-further apple tree!

When

In early spring or fall for deciduous plants; spring is best for evergreens.

Why

If you have lots of time—sometimes a year or longer—to wait, but not a lot to invest in daily maintaining, and want a very low-risk way to propagate your plant, layering is a great way to do it. Because the stem you are propagating is still attached to the parent plant, there is very little chance of it drying out or not getting the food it needs. This technique also requires no special tools or equipment.

Who

Layering works well for many plants and most varieties of shrubs and trees, such as apple, beauty bush, blueberry, bougainvillea, camellia, cotoneaster, daphne, euonymus, filbert, forsythia, fothergilla, hibiscus, holly, honeysuckle, hydrangea, gooseberry, grape, jasmine, lavender, lilac, magnolia, mulberry, oleander, passionflower, pear, rose, tree peony, viburnum, waxflower, weigela, winter sweet, and witch hazel. Air layering is a good technique to use for woody houseplants such as dieffenbachia, dracaena, fiddle-leaf fig, philodendron, and rubber plant.

Difficulty

Simple layering is easy; air layering is only slightly
more difficult. Neither require any special tools or
rooting hormone.

Glossary

aerial roots: Roots that grow into the air rather than in
the ground. These can have different purposes, such as
helping to stabilize the plant, helping it with
nourishment or gas exchanges, or for propagation.

clone: A plant that is genetically identical to its parent
plant because it was propagated asexually.

CROWN
DIVISION

CROWN DIVISION

Summer Lily Mystery

ELLEN

My parents' house was in the middle of a row of century-old Victorians. The house next door had a plant under the bay window, on the shady north side, that my mother called "the summer lily." It put up a flower spike each August with white blossoms, small, not very showy, but, ah, the fragrance. How I love that smell. It takes me right back to long summers, the climbing tree, campouts in the backyard with Dad showing us Cassiopeia and the Pleiades, and praying mantises stalking through the phlox bed. In 1890, one builder built three houses in a row on the west side of High Street. You can tell they were built at the same time because even though each house is different, they all have characteristics that match. Each has a big wraparound porch with turned posts and gingerbread trim; a staircase just inside the front entrance that steps up to a landing lit by a stained glass window; and one bay window facing east in the living room with another facing north in the dining room. Two of the three have slate-roofed barns—carriage houses, really—with a loft for hay and stalls for two horses. When my parents bought the middle house for $6,000 in 1948, it came with an indoor bathroom installed in a room with a window overlooking the porch roof, directly over the paneled front door, and a cat named Thomas Felinus.

The house on the north belonged to "Aunt" Turrie, of award-winning dahlia fame, and the house to the south was where Doc Miller lived with his wife and his daughter, Patricia, who gave me her outgrown sweaters. Doc Miller was called Doc because his father, who had previously lived in that house, really *was* a doctor and the old-timers remembered.

Doc was more interested in green and trim, clean and tidy, than he was in garden profusion, and his manicured lawn stretched from the back-porch grape arbor to the barn. The greensward was broken only by the well-worn path that now led to nowhere but a rosebush (the outhouse had yielded to progress), and by the inch-wide holes the sand hornets dug every summer. His war with the sand hornets was ongoing. He grew colorful but tidy zinnias in the bed between our backyards. He kept the house freshly painted red with white trim, a showpiece among the other houses with more relaxed occupants.

The only place rather out of control was the north side of his house and the narrow strip of land beside it. Those weathered surfaces would hold neither paint nor grass. Every year or two, the red paint peeled up and curled, and the Todd boys, two old brothers with a painting business, would come with their ladders to scrape the wood and give it another coat of paint.

Grass couldn't grow in the strip of soil where the sun didn't reach—only moss and three leafy summer lilies. I could keep an eye on the summer lilies because I spent a lot of time playing in the cave-like space under the wild, arching green branches of the forsythia bush just over our side of the property line between the two houses. There was no fence, but we knew where it was.

Doc liked to put a reclining lawn chair on the backyard grass and sit out there in the hot New Jersey summer sun. With brown skin and a wide grin, he held his arm next to my blonde dad's pink and white one, and chortled over the obvious dark and light, like game pieces of a chess set. Doc loved to tan.

Dad, on the other hand, loved cool and shade. When the air got too hot to sleep in the house, my dad would spread a tarp over the grass of our somewhat scruffier backyard, between the rhubarb and hollyhocks, the phlox and the tansy, and we would lie out there, watching fireflies and bats, and learning the constellations of stars before we all fell asleep in the relative cool of the evening. This was the time of year the summer lilies bloomed.

I noticed the scent from my imaginary playhouse under the forsythia, full and sweet, and a little fruity, wafting on the summer air. It drew me like a bee across the invisible boundary to the plants. One of those three plants with the ordinary-looking green leaves had put up a flower stalk and made inconsequential-looking (I thought) white flowers. They weren't big like the lilies that appeared at Easter alongside my new hat I would wear to the sunrise service Dad and I hiked to on Cokesbury Hill. They weren't interesting like the orange tiger lilies in the front yard, with their recurving petals and sepals, their black spots (I thought they should have stripes), and the shiny black bulbils growing in the leaf axils. They didn't cover swaths of countryside like the wild daylilies along the back roads.

But, inconsequential or not, the smell of those little white flowers would let you skip a rung on Jacob's ladder and cause the angels to compose as well as sing. I ran to get Mother so I could bask in her pleasure as well as my own.

Decades later, I smelled the very same scent 2,000 miles away from the original, in my neighbor's backyard. It came from a hosta in bloom that grew by my neighbor's back steps. So now I know what the summer lily is, and I hope I can talk my neighbor into giving me a crown cutting.

Sand Hornets

Locally called sand hornets, commonly called cicada killers, these big solitary wasps prey on annual eastern cicadas. They nest in inch-wide holes that they dig in barren areas, the sides of gravel roads, and lawns like Doc Miller's. You can see adults flying low over areas looking for a good place to excavate. The females do the digging, and they really get into it. Their holes are 10–20 inches long with side tunnels. They make a fair-size sand pile by biting off a bit of soil then kicking it out of the tunnel with their hind feet. Their next job is to catch a cicada, which they paralyze by stinging—pretty much the only thing they *do* sting. They carry it home, put it in a side tunnel, and lay one egg on it. Then they go hunt another cicada. Adult sand hornets live all summer, until September. The next year, males emerge first. They cannot sting, but rather fly to tops of hills and wait for the females, wrestling in the air as they defend their territory.

Cast Concrete Hosta Leaves

This is a fun way to preserve the sculptural beauty of a hosta leaf and create an organic-looking stepping stone for the garden.

ONE

Select a leaf and lightly coat its veined underside with vegetable oil.

TWO

In a box large enough to lay the leaf out, mound up some slightly damp sand and lay the leaf over it, veined side (i.e., bottom side) up. Dampening the sand will allow you to shape the mound and keep the cement curing even. Mounding the sand will allow the leaf to be cast in its natural curve. Using a box will make cleanup easier.

THREE

Mix up one part portland cement to one part sand, adding water until it feels like a nice, thick mud. Follow the package directions; most require the mixed cement to sit for 10 minutes before it is ready to be used.

FOUR

Wearing gloves, pat handfuls of cement over the leaf, beginning in the middle and working towards the edges, making sure there are no air bubbles. Build up the center until it is $1-1^1/_2$ inches thick, and the edges are $^3/_4-1$ inch thick. The larger the leaf, the thicker the layer of cement will need to be.

FIVE

Smooth the cement, cover it with a layer of plastic, and then let it cure for 24 hours. At this point, you can turn the casting over and peel off the leaf. Let the casting continue to harden and dry for another week before placing it in the garden.

How

Crown division is how you divide plants with multiple stems coming out of the ground, and it is very simple.

ONE

Give the plant you intend to divide a good watering the night before. Not only will this help the plant be less stressed as you're moving it around, but it will also soften the soil, making it easier to get your shovel into.

TWO

Using a shovel, dig all the way around the parent plant, digging a little deeper than the general root mass.

THREE

Gently lift it out of the ground with as many roots intact as possible. Using your shovel, hands, a gardening knife, or whatever works, split the plant into as many portions as you hope to grow. Make sure each portion has roots connected to a bit of crown with at least two or three growth buds.

FOUR

Quickly, so the roots don't dry out, replant the divided pieces at the same depth as they were originally, and give them a nice drink.

Note: If you don't want to dig up the whole plant, you can simply slice off portions; take just a half, or smaller cuttings from the edges, and follow the same steps as above.

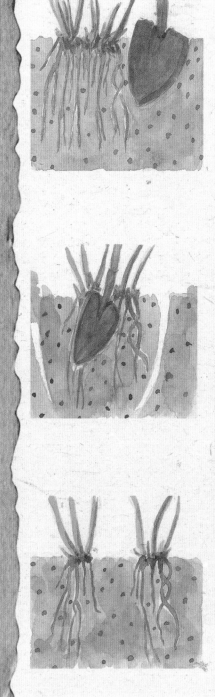

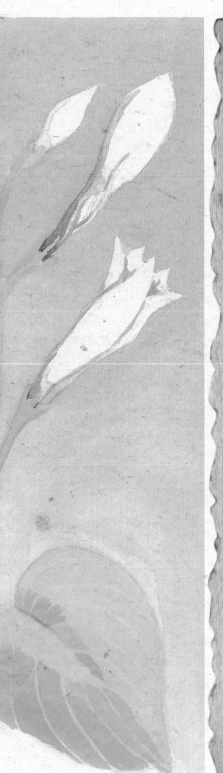

When

The best times are while the plant is dormant—early spring and late fall—but depending on the kind and size of parent plant, other times of the year may work. We've successfully divided plants such as chive and oregano while they were in full bloom.

Why

The plants this will work for often benefit from this activity anyway, and some even require dividing to be kept at their healthiest. Many perennials grow quickly into lovely mounds or clumps, but if they get overcrowded, they may produce fewer or smaller blossoms, or their centers can die back and leave an empty hole. Because many perennials can overgrow their intended area, this is also a way to keep their size in check. But if you don't want to reduce the size of the parent plant, taking a small cutting from the edge of the plant will make it so you don't even need to dig up the whole thing. Just make sure you get it back in the ground fairly quickly, and you're unlikely to have any trouble.

Who

Mature perennial plants that have multistemmed or crowns: aster, astilbe, bee balm, black-eyed Susan, blanketflower, chrysanthemum, clustered bellflowers, coreopsis, daisy, daylily, hosta, lamb's ears, peony, phlox, purple coneflower, yarrow, and many others.

Difficulty

Easy.

Glossary

crown: The part of the plant that is aboveground (i.e., the stems, branches, leaves, flowers, etc., are all part of the plant's crown).

ROOT
DIVISION

ROOT DIVISION

A Horseradish for the Generations

JOHANNA

I've reviewed these facts with my family, and many of them are not true. I might extrapolate to say, much of what I know of my childhood is not true.

There is a long-standing, but sporadic, test of hot machismo in my family: the horseradish connection. At its most fierce, it was my brothers who sustained the tradition, challenging each other to eat an entire spoonful of plain fresh horseradish. We would have tissues handy as their faces reddened, the tears started to run, and liquid flowed freely from their noses. Ah, the fun we have tormenting our bodies when we are young. I might go so far as to say it began with Granddad, unbeknownst to him. Granddad was a notoriously unadventurous eater who had horseradish growing behind the barn. Reportedly, he never got rid of it (As if he could! Consider yourself winked at, fellow horseradish growers.), but, also reportedly, he never ate it.

My granddad had a hard chest and a squishy, gray-bristled cheek. When we would arrive to visit—summer evenings, nine of us piling out of the black Suburban after a twelve-hour drive—he and my grandmother would come outside onto the porch with their arms open, and we would leap and scramble like puppies to get our yearly kiss, squeeze, and warm "Hello, honey! Look how much you've grown!" Except when he was dressed up for church or dressed down for swimming, Granddad wore the same thing: a cotton-poly T-shirt that was worn to near-sheer poly-only on the shoulders and upper chest, over a white undershirt. Both were tucked into canvas pants, which were held up by a belt with a heavy railroad buckle. Under his conductor's hat, his hair was, as long as I'd known him, gray and flat-topped, a haircut preference probably acquired during his years of World War II military service as an X-ray technician. It was a haircut he challenged his grandsons to get, promising them five dollars if they would.

His go-to expression—"Boy-o-boy!"—was used equally to express enthusiasm and disgust, but "Whaddaya wanna do that for?" was reserved for the surprised irritation that comes from finding grandkids doing—What? Building dams? Digging holes? Burning stuff? Eating Popsicles from the freezer?—what mischievous kids do, and generally undoing something that had taken doing. Although he must have had long moments of sitting still (there was an S-gauge model train running all around the inside of the barn at grown-up eye level), when we grandkids were there, he was moving firewood with his tractor, moving docks and boats in and out of the water on the cabin side of the lake, moving kids in his VW bus to hikes and adventures usually involving picnics of the pickles and salami-and-mustard sandwiches variety.

My memories of Granddad are inseparable from memories of hot summers at the lake house on one side and the cabin on the other, a twenty-minute canoe ride away. The cabin is in a clearing, thickly layered with scented pine needles, pine roots, and toe-biting granite that pokes out between them. At the far end is the outhouse, and at the near end is the cabana, a small, dim temple that smelled deliciously of musty towels, talcum powder, and bars of ivory soap, where gendered rituals occurred. Unless the males had been ordered to stay on the far side of the lake, and the women of the family in all their jiggling fullness went for a communal skinny dip (a term that is simultaneously accurate and inaccurate in this situation), the cabana was where we changed en masse into and out of bathing suits and occasionally slathered each others' skin with sunscreen.

When evening began to cool, we would cross the lake for dinner back at the house. The kitchen smelled of steamed veggies from the garden, something roasting in the oven, and coffee and old wood. There would be fresh wild blueberry pie for dessert. *(There is no dispute about the veracity of that last fact.)*

My father will say he didn't taste horseradish until a couple years ago at the farmers' market, when he sampled a sweet horseradish jelly on a cracker. He loved it. I'm not sure where my memory of him laughing in hilarity and weeping in pain at the spoonful contest comes from if this is the case.

But the true lover of horseradish amongst my family's menfolk is my eldest brother. It was after mentioning this in a phone conversation with Granddad that my brother opened his mailbox one day to find a package enclosing a length of bare, brown root dug out from behind the barn. He stuck it in the ground, and it's been a part of his family's yard ever since, emerging even after a resodding project covered the original planting location. Granddad has since passed away, so my brother is the custodian of the pungent plant that is now "Granddad's horseradish." Linking three generations already, it may well continue to purge sinuses and enliven family gatherings—on the plate or on the spoon—for uncounted years to come.

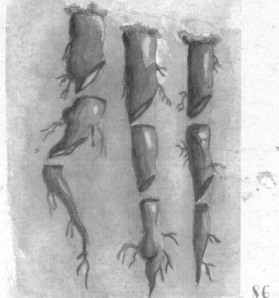

Tip

There's a simple way to keep track of which cut is the up end and which cut is the down end. Make all your top cuts flat (think: flat like the level soil at the top) and all your bottom cuts angled (think: pointy like the tip of the root pointing down). This way you'll always know which end of your root cutting goes which way in the ground.

Growing Horseradish

Horseradish is easy to grow and not too picky about conditions. A tall plant at 2–4 feet, it can give architectural interest to a garden space. Also, it does need room below to grow its long roots. But because it is so eager to provide you with more horseradish, take some care where you plant it and how you dig up the roots; little broken root bits will all grow new plants in the spring. Some gardeners, weary of trying to keep it in a certain area, plant it in a bucket underground to make sure it doesn't outspread its welcome. Many grow it as a perennial at one end of a garden. And unless you eat prime rib every day, whatever you do, don't rototill the area where you've got some horseradish planted.

In the fall, dig up your horseradish roots. To do this, gently lift the soil around the roots, pushing up from below the root with a garden fork. Brush off the dirt and break off any side roots—save them to give away or to replant. You can also leave horseradish in the ground all winter and dig it up in the spring before it has started making leaves. Cut up the root into 1- or 2-inch pieces, making sure there is a little bud on each piece, and making sure the original up/down direction of the root is maintained. Prepare the soil for planting; horseradish thrives in rich composted soil, though it will be content in most soils and conditions. The roots can grow to be as long as 10 inches, so it needs to be loosened deeply. Also, horseradish likes it cool and needs a cold period, but it will still do well where it is hot as long as it can keep its roots moist. Place the root divisions in the soil at a 45-degree angle, up-end up, down-end down. Cover them with soil at least 2 inches, and no more than 5 inches, deep. Give them a good watering; keep them damp until you see leaves start to sprout. Then don't let them dry out, but don't let the roots sit in water. Give horseradish a year until the first harvest; after that, it should be harvested annually.

Horseradish Dip Two Ways

Creamy Horseradish

Although it is pungent enough that if you're shredding a large batch in a food processor, it is recommended to wear goggles and a surgical mask to protect your-self (no, really!), horseradish doesn't bite for very long. It loses its strength imme-diately when it is heated, but also eventually when left at room temperature—after about 20 minutes.

For those who aren't up for eating it straight, horseradish makes a nice dip for crudités or crispy, salty potato chips when diluted with a couple other ingredients. This dip is thick and creamy, and you can make it as pungent as you want by vary-ing the amount of horseradish you include.

2 TO 3 TABLESPOONS FINELY GRATED HORSERADISH

1 CUP SOUR CREAM

JUICE OF 1/2 LEMON

SALT, TO TASTE

Mix together all the ingredients and keep in the fridge. Eat within a week.

Pickley Horseradish

This is an extremely flexible recipe and you should tweak it to the way you like it. Some people enjoy a smooth paste; others prefer a sauce that is thinner and juic-ier. It is often used in a seder dinner as the *maror*, or bitter herbs. It's also nice tucked into mashed potatoes, spread on a sandwich, mixed into a salad vinaigrette, blended into some hummus, served beside breakfast eggs and potato hash, dol-loped on fish, added to deviled eggs . . .

1 POUND HORSERADISH, FINELY GRATED

1/2 CUP WHITE WINE VINEGAR

1 1/2 TEASPOONS SALT

SUGAR, TO TASTE

Mix all the ingredients together, and store in a covered glass jar in the fridge. Keeps for a year.

Horseradish and Religious Symbolism

The Passover seder, a symbolic meal where Jewish families retell the story of Exodus to the next generation and remember God's deliverance of Israel from slavery in Egypt, is designed to engage all five senses. The role of bitter herbs, or *maror* (typically horseradish), in the retelling, is to bring tears to the participant's eyes (and, presumably, nose), as a way of recalling the bitter anguish felt under Pharaoh's rule, so as to remember the goodness and joy of redemption.

Playing a similar role in Polish Easter celebrations, a traditional Polish Easter dish, *bialy barszcz*, known in translation as white borscht, is a tangy, delicious bowlful of Easter symbolism. Like all traditional folk foods, there are as many variations as there are households making it, but in general, it includes potatoes; kielbasa sausage (a symbol of the abundance of both God's mercy and of celebration at the resurrection); hard-boiled egg (a symbol of new life); dairy, such as sour cream and butter (a symbol of the richness of salvation); and horseradish (a symbol of the bitterness of the Passion), which is often, in modern times, added individually to each bowl to suit the eater's taste.

Sarah and Tim Ozimek, "Polish White Borscht (Bialy Barszcz)," *Curious Cuisinière*, April 17, 2014.
Ina Lipkowitz, "'To a worm in horseradish, the whole world is horseradish' (Yiddish Proverb)," *Academy of Food*, March 15, 2013.

How

Root cutting is often done in the season when there aren't a lot of other gardening chores going on, which is one reason it's so satisfying to do. The propagation principles are the same for woody-rooted plants, such as shrubs, as for smaller perennial plants.

ONE

When the plant has gone dormant, remove some of the root, no more than one-third of the total. Lift it out of the ground if it is a smallish perennial. If it is a woody plant, excavate a length of pencil-thick root and clip it off with clean, sharp pruners.

TWO

Replant the parent plant and give it a drink.

THREE

Rinse off the removed roots.

FOUR

Cut the roots into 3- to 6-inch pieces. To keep track of which end of the root is which, cut the end that was closest to the plant in a flat cut, and the end farthest away in a diagonal cut. When it's time to plant, you will know which end goes up: the flat end.

FIVE

Cover the new root cuttings with 2—3 inches of soil, either directly in the garden, or in a pot inside, either keeping the angled cut down, or laying them horizontally. If you are propagating them inside, keep them in a warm, humid spot. Once they've been hardened off (see page 25), they will be ready for planting outside.

When

When the plant is dormant and before it has started to leaf, usually late fall to early spring.

Glossary

dormant: Periods of being alive but not photosynthesizing or actively growing.

Why

For many other species, root division is a low-effort way to get many clones at once. In the case of propagating horseradish, it is the main way, as the plant rarely sets viable seed. But it's also a handy way, because once you have the root, you can hold onto it for a while without planting it. Just keep it in the fridge, wrapped in something to protect it from drying out (but don't let it get moldy) until a good time to plant—spring, summer, or early fall.

Who

Bear's breeches, bishop's hat (*Epimedium*), bleeding heart, bluestar (amsonia), cardoon, comfrey, coneflower, eryngium (sea holly), fig, garden phlox, glory bower (bleeding heart vine; *Clerodendrum thomsoniae*), hollyhock, horseradish, hydrangea, Japanese anemone (also called windflower; *Anemone hupehensis*), Japanese aster, joe-pye weed, lilacs, mock orange, nepeta (catmint), Oregon grape, Oriental poppy, pasque flower (*Pulsatilla vulgaris* and *Anemone pulsatilla*) pussy willow, raspberry, red- and yellow-twig dogwood, rose of Sharon, nongrafted rose, sumac, trumpet vine, weeping willow, and many more.

Difficulty

Easy, with some elbow grease required.

SAVING
CUCURBIT
SEEDS

SAVING CUCURBIT SEEDS

Squash from God

ELLEN

We experienced difficult times in those months after George's job disappeared, and our lives changed. Seemingly little incidents assumed their full importance in those days, and when our friend Rita called to ask, "Would you eat a squash if I brought it over?" her offer seemed important.

I pictured zucchini for supper, but as it turned out, I pictured wrong. A few minutes later, Rita tapped on our door, tall and friendly, a hard winter squash in each arm. One was round, the size of a milk jug; the other long, the size of a baby. Smooth pink skin, slightly pinker than my own, covered them from stem to nether regions, and in spite of their dissimilar shapes, both sported delicately gold-bordered robin's-egg-blue bottoms. I was mesmerized.

"Can I put them down?" Rita pleaded.

"Of course!" I replied, coming back to the moment. But I had to ask, wide eyed, "What *are* those?"

"Squash from God," Rita replied matter of factly. I had certainly never seen them in seed catalogs or in the grocery store. And she had brought them just when we needed them. "One day, a plant just sprang up out of my garden," she explained. "It grew and grew until it covered the whole ten-foot fence between our yard and the school ground, and then it

96

began producing big blue balls and long things hanging there on the fence. Gradually over the course of the summer, they turned pink. They were squash! We tried one and it was very good. Every year, I save seeds from the squash, dry them, and plant them the next spring. And every year, the squash grow in different shapes. But they are always blue and pink, and they always taste good."

We cut the round one open and found thick flesh of a glorious orange, the color of egg yolks from free-range chickens. We steamed, we sautéed, we casseroled, we souped. They tasted fresh and slightly nutty, and seemed to work equally well as an ingredient in recipes or as a vegetable dish. They were good food in generous quantity.

Each squash held many seeds, too woody to roast and munch, but easy to dry and save. I saved a bowlful and, the next spring, planted several hills of seeds beside our backyard fence. After a week, I spotted seed leaves rising from the soil.

Each year I replant Squash from God, and each fall, I give some away. Rita remains my friend, although she moved away from her old garden to a new town, and last year I even gave her a squash—a beautiful pumpkin-shaped blue one. It sat on her porch until it turned pink with a blue bum, and she ate it and saved the seeds. She'll be thinking of me this summer when her vines reach out.

Gary's Roasted Squash Soup

SERVES 8 TO 10

1/4 CUP OLIVE OIL

2 HEADS GARLIC, PEELED

3 MEDIUM ONIONS, PEELED AND CHOPPED INTO 1-INCH PIECES

3 LARGE CARROTS, PEELED AND CHOPPED INTO 1-INCH PIECES

2 CELERY RIBS, CHOPPED INTO 1-INCH LENGTHS

8 CUPS (ABOUT 4 POUNDS) WINTER SQUASH (SUCH AS TURBAN OR BUTTERNUT), PEELED, CLEANED, AND CUT INTO 1-INCH PIECES

3 TABLESPOONS CHOPPED FRESH HERBS (SUCH AS SAGE, PARSLEY, OR BASIL), DIVIDED, OR A PINCH OF DRY HERBS (SUCH AS ITALIAN HERBS OR HERBES DE PROVENCE)

6 CUPS CHICKEN OR VEGETABLE BROTH

3/4 CUP CREAM, DIVIDED

BOUILLON POWDER (OPTIONAL)

SALT AND PEPPER, TO TASTE

Preheat oven to 350 degrees F. In a baking pan, drizzle the olive oil over the garlic, onions, carrots, celery, squash, and 2 tablespoons of the herbs. Toss together until they are all evenly coated. Spread the oiled, seasoned vegetables in the pan and cover with aluminum foil. Roast in oven for 1 hour, or until vegetables are soft and slightly caramelized. Let cool.

Purée the soup, either in a blender or with an immersion blender, using the chicken or vegetable broth as liquid. If using a blender, work in batches. At this point, the soup can be stored in the fridge for 1 day, or it can be finished immediately.

To finish, put the soup into a pot and bring to a simmer. Turn off the heat and gently stir in 1/2 cup of the cream. Season to taste with bouillon and salt and pepper.

To serve, transfer the soup to a tureen or to individual bowls. Garnish with a drizzle of cream and a sprinkle of the remaining herbs.

We are not the only ones to notice that squash is open to change. New England poet Robert Francis (1901–87) alludes to open-pollinated squash in two verses of his poem "Squash in Blossom":

How lush, how loose, the uninhibited squash is.

If ever hearts (and these immoderate leaves

Are vegetable hearts) were worn on sleeves,

The squash's are. In green the squash vine gushes.

The flowers are cornucopias of summer,

Briefly exuberant and cheaply golden.

And if they make a show of being hidden,

Are open promiscuously to every comer.

How

Quirky Squash from God surprises us each year because we never know what the next crop will look like. Squash easily crosses with other varieties of squash, and even with other vine plants like cucumbers, melons, and pumpkins. The offspring of our vines—in other words, next year's squash—can exhibit characteristics of those outcrossing plants. For instance, our squash may be as small as a grapefruit on one vine, or as large as a big pumpkin on another; pink or blue; and round or long, all depending on the previous year's pollen. When Rita and I save our squash seeds for the next year, we know we are saving romance, intrigue, and mystery.

The actual saving part of collecting squash seeds is easy. I open a mature Squash from God, scrape out the seeds and the stringy, gooey endocarp, separate the seeds from the goop with my fingers, and put them in a pie plate on my counter to dry.

Each day I turn them and stir them to expose the seeds underneath to the air. They must dry thoroughly. When they feel light and dry, and make a rattling sound as they drop back into the pan, I put them in a canning jar, screw on the lid, and store them in the fridge until planting time next spring.

If you want to keep the same known variety—such as crookneck, or pattypan, or turban—next year, getting to the saving part takes some attention but is actually pretty simple. Squash plants grow both male and female flowers; the male flowers have longish, slender stems, and the female flowers grow on top of tiny, round, green squash-like balls. You have to isolate each to make sure the selected male pollinates the chosen squash blossom.

Here is how to go about isolating and pollinating:

ONE

The night before the mating is to take place, determine which flower buds will open the next day. They will be light yellow, rather than green, and their tips will be pointed.

TWO

If you are working with a small-flowered variety, you can slip a paper clip over the buds to prevent them from opening. If you grow a large-flowered squash, you will need to hold the bud closed with a rubber band or tie a plastic bag around it. These flowers open with the new day, so in the morning, pick the male flower and touch its pollen-loaded anthers, found in the center of the bloom, to the moist stigma in the center of the female flower. Make sure some of the pollen from the male now sits on the top of the stigma of the female.

THREE

Close the female flower back up again with a clip or rubber band so bees cannot bring more pollen to it from another garden, and tuck the male flower behind your ear for fun. Be sure to mark that particular female flower with a tag so you can grow its squash to full maturity and save those seeds. Full maturity is key for viable seeds. Sturdy winter squash automatically opens to mature seeds because the hard epicarp, or rind, that indicates good ability to withstand winter storage also indicates complete development. On the other hand, we eat tender summer squash before it is technically ripe. Let your tagged squash develop on the vine until the skin is hard and the fruit is very ripe. Then you can separate out the seeds, dry and label them, and save them, covered in the refrigerator, to plant the next spring.

When

Most cucurbits like a soil temperature of at least 65 degrees F to germinate, and hotter is better, so most often they are started inside while it is still cool and transplanted outdoors for the hot season.

Why

For Cucurbitaceae plants, this kind of controlled pollinating is the only way to maintain the genetic sameness in seeds of a family favorite. Why maintain a family favorite? Because it tastes good. Also, plant breeding is fun.

Who

Members of the Cucurbitaceae family, which includes melons, cucumbers, winter squash, summer squash, pumpkins, gourds, and loofahs.

Difficulty

Intermediate.

Glossary

endocarp: The stringy, gooey, uneaten part of a squash that holds and surrounds the seeds in the middle.

to cross/outcrossing: To breed a plant (or animal, for that matter) with one not closely related to it.

anthers: The part of the flower that carries the pollen, usually found at the tip of a slender, stem-like stalk in the center of the male squash blossom.

stigma: Surrounded by petals, the stigma is the raised yellow structure in the center of the female blossom.

pollen: A fine yellow powder; each grain contains the plant's male DNA information.

Do squash seeds *have* to be stored in the fridge? No. They will not become less viable simply because they are stored at ambient temperature. But their chances of staying healthy enough to grow are increased when they are stored somewhere cool, dark, and dry, and the temperature and humidity levels they are stored at remain constant. For most people, this is in their fridge or freezer. Of the two—cool and dry—dry is the more important.

Hick Mystic

I look for discernable strands of story
in the bits of soapsuds still
in your hands after washing up;
whole palm readings require
a feather from a freshly killed bird

I'll make you tea from the loose-leaf
whose house powers are unknown and
draw predictions from my shoebox oracle

I see into the future with the large squash
in my backyard so full with seeds of possibility
right now that you are bound to end up
happy in one dimension or another

I don't own tarot cards but
last night's gin rummy was in your favor and
though I have never been able to
make much of planet alignments
I do insist on a cosmic calendar that
affects us more than we'd like to say and
just how is sometimes embarrassing

Rebecca Buchert

Rebecca Buchert, *Hick Mystic*, copyright 2016.

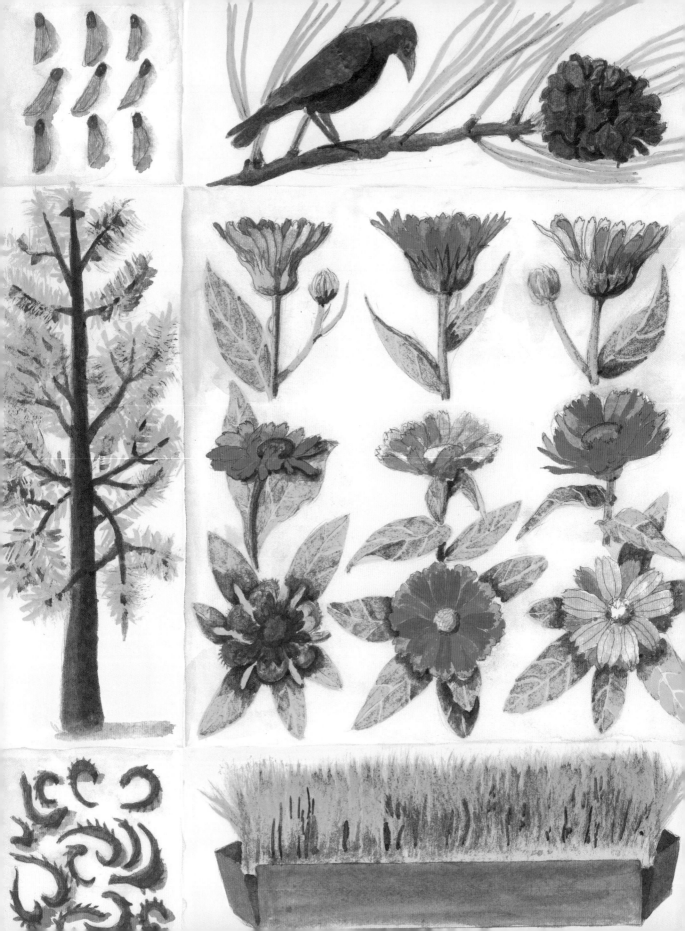

SIMPLE
SEED
SAVING

SIMPLE SEED SAVING

A Calendula Shortcut to Community

JOHANNA

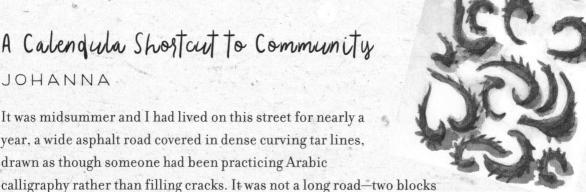

It was midsummer and I had lived on this street for nearly a
year, a wide asphalt road covered in dense curving tar lines,
drawn as though someone had been practicing Arabic
calligraphy rather than filling cracks. It was not a long road—two blocks
or so—and was bookended by a busy street on one end (we lived on *that* side of it) and
a quiet T-intersection at the other. Except where someone had knocked down one of the
houses to put up a dreary gray cement-brick fourplex, the homes on either side were
variations on the dark-brick postwar bungalow, set back from the road, a mature tree in
front, and fences of all varieties between each. I walked slowly down the uneven sidewalk,
my eye coming to rest on the back of a small woman in a headscarf a few houses away. She
was bent over an unruly side bed, masses of colors clumped around her, some nearly as tall
as her doubled-over frame.

As I got closer, she straightened. Some dark gray hair was curling out from the sides of
her kerchief. Turning around, she looked directly at me as I walked up. She had a pair of
pruning scissors in her hand, and there was a woven gardening basket on the ground near
her feet. Holding my gaze, she held out her hand to me. Without too much consideration, I
held out my own and found it filled with a small pile of brown seeds, curved and bumpy,
uneven in length. "I am Astrid," she said in a light accent. "Do you know calendula?" She
pointed to the tangerine blooms around her knees, cheery, vibrant orange and yellow
blooms on sturdy stems with small rounded leaves beneath them. I hadn't, but now I knew
both calendula *and* Astrid.

What is it that makes you feel part of a community, part of a neighborhood? How is it
that sometimes you can live somewhere for years before starting to feel like you belong? At
that moment, the light handful of friendship I was holding was like an abbreviation to

belonging on this street, in my new neighborhood. I felt as if I were holding something rare, something precious and difficult to come by. Only later did I learn how generous calendula is in sharing its joyful seed. Although it wasn't as rare as I'd thought, it was definitely still as precious as it seemed. I've grown Astrid's calendula at three different homes since, and passed along handfuls of seeds to other friends and strangers in need of belonging. I not only got to *know* calendula, but I have fallen in love with it and have collected as many varieties as I can find to grow in my garden.

The Legend of the Potawatomi Plum

JOHANNA

As told to me by someone who heard it nearly from the original source, more or less.

A wagon train of pioneers was headed west across the Great Plains. Through the trials and deprivations, a young man and a young woman fell in love. They knew the chances of their making it all the way to the West together unscathed were uncertain; they wanted to be wed immediately so as to seal their commitment to each other while they still could. But what to do for a ring? Such things as could be had from others had been left behind or used for bartering along the way. So then, what symbol to use to publish their vow? In a grove near a river, out in the wide prairie, they stood beneath a wild plum tree, and exchanging vows of faithfulness, each held in their fingers a deep purple plum to the lips of the other till their teeth had split the skin and juice ran down to their wrists. Then, sucking the pits till they were clean, the couple exchanged plum pits, the promise of a future together. Their anxiety over reaching the West together had been well founded, and not too much later, an accident left the young man dead and the young woman maimed— missing parts of both legs. But her vision of a promised land across the Rocky Mountains, and her love of the man whose plum pit she carried sewed into the bodice of her dress, propelled her forward. At last she reached a fertile valley, a place of rest after such a treacherous journey. She settled and established a homestead. And in a sheltered part of her property, the young woman tenderly planted and tended the nuptial Potawatomi plum. It still grows today, gnarled and knobby, and every summer it drips with round, juicy balls of plummy tartness, a monument to the passion of man and grit of woman. And younger trees, grown every year from its generous pits, are found in warm valleys all over the West.

Saving Tree Seeds

ELLEN

The first time I went seed collecting with George, he and the man who would become his major professor for a master's degree were checking each other out. The great changes in any society come from the inside out, and a great change was incubating in the mind of the head of our family. As he worked at his student job as a lab assistant for Dr. Wang, a professor of forest genetics, George gradually realized he really was more interested in forest genetics than he was in forest management. He listened to romantic stories of Dr. Wang's youthful botanizing trips through the mountains of southern China with only a backpack and a mule for support during weeks in the forest. He admired the fact that Dr. Wang had a tree species, *Pinus wangii*, named after him—recognition for his labor. He began to hope that Dr. Wang would accept him as a student and start him on the path to a PhD.

Dr. Wang, on the other hand, saw a handsome, blond young man with not-so-good undergraduate grades, but with a keen intellect for grasping new ideas and growing interest in the possibilities of research. George had a willingness to meticulously carry out tedious lab jobs such as counting needle numbers in fascicles (do ponderosa pines *really* always have three needles in those little bundles?), measuring fascicle lengths, and counting the number of whorls in the Fibonacci spirals on the cones. And . . . George was the possessor of a valid Idaho driver's license. Dr. Wang's graduate students were all from Taiwan, and they needed a driver. George often joked that it was the driver's license that got him into graduate school.

Dr. Wang was looking for variability within ponderosa pine to map where trees with various characteristics grew. He wanted to sort out environmental differences from trees that were different because of genetic control. This meant he needed collections of seeds from disparate areas—Lake Tahoe; Yosemite; King's Canyon; Sequoia National Park; an isolated pocket of trees, a remnant of glaciation, in North Dakota; the Lost Forest in Central Oregon; and trees from a big army base in western Washington. When George was on assignment to gather seed-filled ponderosa pinecones from around Lake Tahoe, our little boy, Charlie, and I went with him.

We drove south from Idaho's panhandle to Interstate 80 then west across Nevada's basin and rangeland until, at last, we saw a small road off to the south that the map said led to Lake Tahoe. We drove up a mountain, reached the top, and got out to look. Behind us: bare ground, sagebrush, juniper, prickly pear, piñon pine, and a shimmer on the road, a mirage of water. Before us, the real thing: a blue jewel, like a round piece of sky, beautiful Lake Tahoe in the hollow of the hills, and a lush green hillside with tall sugar pine and ponderosa pine, and my first site of manzanita with its lovely reddish curling bark. The rain shadow, caused by the clouds from the west colliding with the mountain above the lake to drop their rain, provided enough water to grow a lush forest community. Even the rocks and soil there are amiably granitic—an acid forest soil perfect for ponderosa. The houses that now surround Lake Tahoe had not yet been built, and we pitched our tent in a flat, shady glade with no thought of being disturbed by people.

The next day, George climbed trees and tossed down cones—ripe but still closed with pitch. Charlie and I packed them stickily, tree by tree, into meticulously labeled muslin bags, where they would dry and open back in the lab.

Well, George *did* get into graduate school, he *did* earn a PhD, and he had a long and interesting career as a research scientist. He never lost his admiration for Dr. Wang. And Dr. Wang, for four good years, got himself and his students a blue-eyed, good-natured, all-American driver.

Home Turf

JOHANNA

Green is the stuff of life, and in beginning a new life by getting married, we had the tables decorated with a green that to us felt modern but warm and earthy: wheatgrass. It was a winter wedding, right before Christmas. The florist grew the wheatgrass in big flats and cut it out like carpet to lay in the long, narrow galvanized-steel chick feeders I had bought to display them in. Red ranunculi on tall, curving stems in mismatched glass containers were the counterpoint.

Because we got married in a small town a couple hours travel for everyone who was attending and our ceremony was in the morning, we had friends help the professionals set up the town hall where our reception luncheon would be held. I had no idea how beautiful it would be, and it was a lovely surprise to walk into, all white and red and green, the yellow winter light coming through the windows and reflecting through the vases, and best of all, the loving, supportive faces of most of the people who meant the most to us in the world.

For the next four years, I grew wheatgrass for our anniversaries. It was something bright and alive and thriving in cold mid-December, in midtransition, in the heart of difficult years of demanding professional training and lengthy commuting, when sometimes we had to really search to find the places our roots twined together.

But the tough, matting, white roots were forming a layer of dense, hopefully impenetrable support under the soil for all the vibrant, green life above, and we welcomed to our family a daughter. In prepping the nest, out came the silvery, galvanized trays. It felt a little odd to be setting them up in the spring, but our family's addition to the millennia of symbols accorded to wheat had been set.

Like everyone does, we fell hard for our firstborn. Even brand new, she was wondrous, perceptive, responsive, delicate and strong, willful, beautiful. Her first birthday was as big a milestone of ours as it was of hers. We would be one-year-old parents. A few weeks before the date, I pulled out the long, narrow, galvanized-steel trays. There were fewer of them, as some of the trays had been pillaged to use in my new chicken setup out behind the house, so I added tin cans we had emptied as we fed our family, to give as party favors.

Our first son was born a year after that, a golden boy, round and scrumptious as a plump wheat berry. We were weeks away from an intercontinental move and a new job. The chickens and all their gear had been given away; the wheatgrass may or may not have been grown. To be honest, I can't remember. It was a busy time.

Over the next few years, our tradition made spotty appearances. Sometimes the wheat seeds were sown *on* the commemorative event, sometimes weeks later, and sometimes forgotten entirely but never permanently; the symbol had grown too dear for that. The most recent planting, a freehanded one that turned the backyard sandbox into a dense forest for the resident truck fleet, was joyously, and liberally, planted by our third child, a boy as sunny as summer and bright as morning. Still warm, still earthy, still beautiful, wheatgrass continues to celebrate our favorite, hardest work: growing and building our family.

Make Your Own Seed Envelope

Sharing seeds in a beautiful envelope you've created adds a layer of personality and charm to a botanical gift. Turn to page 144 for a template you can trace onto cardstock and use to create seed envelopes out of any beautiful or interesting paper you choose, including repurposed artwork, magazines, catalogs, and books. Or keep the paper simple and draw on it yourself. Just make sure to include somewhere the details of why these seeds matter to you, the year you collected them, and where. We've also made one for you, ready to print out and make, no template needed, at ellensheppardbuchert.com. We hope it will help inspire you to collect and share your own seeds.

Sterile Hybrids

If you find your seeds aren't growing the same plant you collected them from, you may have a hybrid on your hands. Hybrids are plants that have been bred professionally under controlled circumstances from two different varieties of the same species to produce certain desirable traits. Unfortunately, most often these traits will not be expressed in the next generation, they may gradually disappear over several generations, or the seeds may be sterile and not grow at all. Open-pollinated plants, on the other hand, are pollinated by the same species of the same plant and tend to change characteristics slowly. Heirloom plants are all open pollinated. They are also, by definition, older, with characteristics that have remained pretty much unchanged for several generations.

Avocado Pit Ink

By Patricia Lenhardt
facebook.com/PeddleryPressandFiberworks

Dipping a quill or pen into a bottle of ink may seem a bit old fashioned, but it can be a fun art project for the kids or for you. Because you're producing only a small amount of ink—about 3 or 4 ounces—it doesn't take a lot of plant material or time. You will need only a few specialty items from the craft store or dye supplier to make the ink last longer and not fade quickly.

Mordant *Most natural inks require a mordant to bind the dye to the paper fibers and retain lightfastness. Mordants are generally tannins or mineral salts. Soda ash, also known as washing soda or sodium carbonate, is an alkaline mordant. The most common and safest mordants are alum and iron; each will bring out a different color from the avocado seeds. Iron can be obtained by boiling the ink in an iron skillet or adding a rusty piece of iron to the pot.*

Gum arabic *This is used to thicken the liquid. It helps the ink flow onto the paper in a controlled fashion and binds the ink with the paper. It will also help preserve the color.*

Thyme essential oil *This is used to help prevent mold from forming in the ink.*

2 FRESH LARGE AVOCADO PITS, CHOPPED INTO SMALL PIECES

1 CUP WATER

1 TEASPOON SODA ASH

1/2 TEASPOON GUM ARABIC

3 DROPS THYME ESSENTIAL OIL

Simmer the avocado pits and soda ash in the water for 20 minutes. Strain out the pits and whisk in the gum arabic while the ink is still warm so it dissolves easily. Cool and pour into a small bottle. Add the thyme oil and shake to mix. The ink is ready to use for writing or drawing. Store it in a bottle with a tight-sealing lid in a cool, dark place.

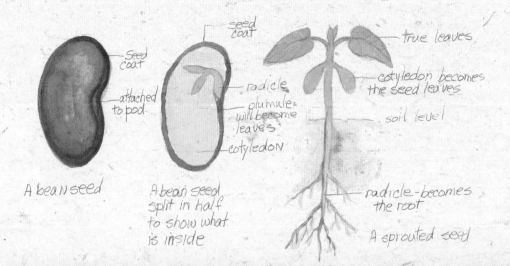

seed coat

true leaves

seed coat

cotyledon becomes the seed leaves

radicle

attached to pod

plumule will become leaves

soil level

cotyledon

A bean seed

A bean seed split in half to show what is inside

radicle—becomes the root

A sprouted seed

My Sister's Raw Almond Pesto

Pesto is traditionally made with seeds from the piñon pine (pine nuts, or piñon nuts), but it is delicious made with seeds from other plants too. Any portion of the almonds can be substituted with other kinds of nuts or nutty seeds, especially pumpkin and sunflower, with delicious results. This variation is wonderful on pretty much anything: crackers, toast, veggies, or even in place of mayo on sandwiches. It also makes a great base for salad dressing; just get it to a pourable consistency with yogurt for a creamy dressing, or oil and vinegar for a vinaigrette.

$1^1/_2$ CUP RAW ALMONDS, SOAKED FOR AT LEAST 6 HOURS

1 CUP FRESH BASIL LEAVES

$^1/_4$ CUP CHOPPED GREEN ONIONS

2 TABLESPOONS LEMON JUICE

ZEST OF 1 LEMON

PINCH OF RED PEPPER FLAKES

SALT, TO TASTE

$^1/_2$ CUP CANOLA OIL, PLUS MORE AS NEEDED

Add all the ingredients, except for the water, to the blender and begin to process, adding more oil as needed to allow it to blend smoothly. It should be tangy, salty, and creamy. Store it in the fridge and use it within 3–4 days.

How

There are general principles to simple seed saving, and they truly are simple. This guide gives those general principles. Understanding a few specifics about the plant you're working with will help you recognize different phases of its life cycle or any particulars required for germination, but gathering seeds is one of the simplest and most exciting ways to grow beautiful plants that keep alive memories or the associations you have with them and share them with the people you love.

Collecting Cosmos Seeds

ONE

Although cosmos will produce tangerine clouds of flowers over their delicate, fernlike leaves if you deadhead the spent blooms regularly, you need to leave some of the flowers to grow to maturity if you'd like seeds. This means that you'll let the petals wither and fall off, which they will do once the flower has been pollinated. The base of the flower will start to swell as a seedhead starts to form. Wait for the seeds to dry out completely. You'll know they're ready when, like a dramatic fireworks display, they pop out sea urchin style in all directions. It's as wonderful as the flower itself, but difficult to display; the seeds knock off easily when they are dry and ready to harvest. One way of making sure you get them before the birds do is to snip off the almost-dry seedheads and put them upside down in a paper bag somewhere where they can continue drying. But cosmos, like calendula, is generous with blossom and seed, so if you only end up with a few, plant them. Within a growing season, you'll have access to a generation of many more seeds.

TWO

Once you have collected the dry seeds, keep them dry in a jar or envelope, and store them somewhere where the temperature and humidity levels will remain fairly constant.

THREE

Warmth and moisture are required to germinate most seeds, including cosmos; in 5—10 days, they will have sprouted and started on their way to producing the next generation of seeds.

Why

You want to bring home a tiny, portable souvenir from a special trip; seeds are easy to carry. You want to send a bit of last summer's family reunion to each of your grandchildren; seeds can be kept viable over long periods and distances. You want to keep alive the flavors and textures of a plant that only your family has grown for the past several generations; seeds will preserve all the distinct genetic variabilities that are encoded only in that plant.

Who

Most heirloom annuals and perennials, wildflowers, many garden vegetables, some trees, most edible and flowering annuals, herbs, and all cereal grains. Please note that some seeds require various treatments to grow well once they've been harvested (e.g., they need to be chilled for a certain amount of time, or they need to be soaked to germinate well), but what distinguishes this kind of propagation technique is the ease with which you can *collect* the seeds. Once you're convinced of the fun of doing that, you can look up individual plants to see what particular needs they have for sprouting.

Difficulty

Easy.

The Secret Math of Plants

What do pinecones, pineapples, and palm trees have in common? A spiraling series of numbers that underlies plant growth, and much of the natural world (including your own body!), known as the Fibonacci sequence. It's elegantly simple: 0, 1, 1, 2, 3, 5, 8, 13, 21, 34, . . . and is made by adding the previous two numbers together to get the next number in the sequence. Count the number of petals on each flower in your bouquet. Most likely, they are Fibonacci numbers. Cut a red cabbage across its equator: see the Fibonacci spiral? Look from the top down at a growing sunflower. Can you see the leaves growing in a consistent spiraling rotation? Fibonacci again.

You'll find Fibonacci numbers in almost all your plants once you start looking, including the arrangement of seeds in seedheads, the arrangement of leaves on stalks and branches, the number of flower petals, and the way petals spiral out.

BULBS
AND
CORMS

BULBS AND CORMS

Spring of 1966

ELLEN

George and I, baby Charlie, and
our friend Russell all piled into
our blue VW bug and drove from
the University of Idaho campus
to the North Fork of the Clearwater River in
north-central Idaho. We were headed to see the last log drive in
the United States. This run sent timber from the mountains above the Clearwater to the
Potlatch mill in Lewiston. Historically, transporting timber by floating the logs downriver
had been economical, but those dangerous ways of river transport had been replaced by
logging trucks, saving both money and lives. Logging along the Clearwater was the last
holdout of the old ways, and that antiquated operation was being shut down by the
imminent construction of the Dworshak Dam, which would effectively block the river.

As we drove around a curve in the road, we spotted a footbridge crossing the Clearwater.
Curious, we pulled over, crossed the log-floating river on the footbridge, and arrived at an
empty little farmhouse backed by green hills. It was wonderful, like a beautiful but
weathered actress on a stage. But it was the set, not the actress, that took our breath away:
as far as the eye could see, right up those hills and all the way down to the river, were
blooming daffodils waving in the wind.

"When all at once I saw a crowd," said Wordsworth, "a host of golden daffodils . . .
fluttering and dancing in the breeze."

The beloved poem spread out in all reality before us. "Ten thousand saw I at a glance,
tossing their heads in sprightly dance." We stood looking with amazement at the
extraordinary fields of flowers and imagined the joy they must have been to that family,
way out there in the canyon, when winter finally broke and those nodding yellow blooms

were the witness and evidence of spring. We wondered about how long the farm family had to have lived there to allow the bulbs time to divide and naturalize into that great swath of yellow. The breathtaking loveliness, along with the poignant sense of the last of the log drives and the closing of that chapter of American history, and the loss of that farm, fused together as we stood there trying to take in the vision. That day, and those daffodils, planted themselves in our hearts.

The Van der Molen's Crocuses

ELLEN

The Van der Molens lived directly east across the street from us on Browndale Crescent. Past childbearing years but recently married, they radiated industry and purpose. There were four in the household—Mr. and Mrs. Van der Molen, Mrs. Van der Molen's mother, Mrs. Niemeyer, and their tiny, yappy dog, Brownie. Both Van der Molens worked at jobs, and unlike our mom-at-home, seven-child, Siberian husky dog, cat, and raccoon more *casual* establishment, their lawn was trim and green and their windows always clean. Their driveway wore fresh black asphalt, repainted every year, and their car was immaculate. On the east side of the street, rainbows formed over their house in the afternoon after it rained.

Bill Van der Molen had a rare talent. He could find water. Not only could he find it, but he could tell the depth and direction of the flow. Bill told me, "When we moved into this house, I couldn't sleep, it was so close."

"What was so close?" I questioned, thinking he undoubtedly meant the neighbors were so close. The houses were semidetached, as they are called there.

"The water," he answered with a wasn't-it-obvious tone of voice. "It is under our bedroom, about twenty-six feet down, and flowing that way," he said, pointing south toward Toronto and Lake Ontario.

"Did you get used to it?" I asked.

"No. We switched bedrooms with my mother-in-law. There is no water under there. Now we sleep fine, and she doesn't feel it."

"Do you use a dowsing stick?" I asked, remembering my father poking fun at dowsing with a forked apple twig that turned down over the backyard septic tank every time. He thought that very funny.

"I can," he replied, "but I don't need it. It pulls on *me*."

It must have been difficult for you back home in Holland, I thought. Out loud I asked, rather excited by the possibilities, "Do you find water for people? People would pay a lot for that."

"Not very often," he replied. "It takes too much energy. I am tired for weeks afterward and can't go to work. Once in a while," and a twinkle sparked in his eye, "I trade my skills— only to a friend—for a bottle of whiskey."

On more sunny days, little round Mrs. Niemeyer, scarcely taller than her cane, would come out to walk wearing her black rayon dress with the collar. She didn't speak English very well, and I am downright terrible at Dutch, but sometimes I would walk with her and help her a little when she was troubled by "the dizzness." "I have the dizzness today," she would say. They were all worried about the dizzness. The doctor was puzzled by the dizzness.

Dizzy or not, she somehow conveyed the idea that she loved living in Canada, but she missed her husband and the little flowers that grew among the grass in the springtime in the old country. I sympathized. I missed my husband if he was gone for even a week, and I loved flowers.

Maybe they all missed those homey flowers, because one fall, Bill methodically dug careful, tidy holes in his grass and planted crocus bulbs out of a brown box from Holland, all over the front lawn. The flowers came with the spring, picture perfect, evenly spaced. I didn't think much about them until they all appeared at my door in the sweet, tight fist of my passionate little three-year-old, all grassy knees and arms, blond hair tousled and glowing like Mary's halo.

"They are for you, Mommy," she said, with love in her eyes. My breath caught in my chest and my knees—well, I had to bend down anyway to receive the sweet gift and hug the giver. We put the crocuses in a glass and admired their purple freshness.

Later, of course, we had a talk and wrote a note and took it across the street, and of course, we were forgiven. The Van der Molens are grand folks.

The next spring, their yard danced with naturalized crocuses. They looked so pretty, right out of a meadow in Holland. That year, the neighbor children understood ownership; the flowers stayed where they grew. Nobody picked them. Not even one.

Well—maybe one.

To create a spring lawn tapestry of crocus (which technically is a corm, not a bulb), plant species crocus, which bloom two weeks earlier than other larger crocus. Bigger, later bloomers get cut off with the grass before their leaves and flowers mature. Here are a few other tips to help you naturalize crocus in your lawn:

ONE

Select a mostly bright location where the soil is poor and a bit dry.

TWO

In September or October, push your trowel blade through the grass into the soil, and pull back to open a 4-inch-deep wedge of air. Drop in a crocus corm and pull out the trowel, letting the soil and grass close back together again. When all your corms are planted, water the lawn.

THREE

If you are impatient for drifts of flowers, don't be afraid to plant more bulbs.

FOUR

Crocus does best in a chemical-free lawn; no weed killers, no fertilizers.

FIVE

Hold off mowing a little in the spring, and mow to a height setting of 3 inches or longer. This gives the crocus leaves time to mature and nourish the bulb before they are cut.

Bulb and Tube

JOHANNA

In the beginning, there was garlic; the beginning of every dinner, most lunches, and many breakfasts. Since it was added to every soup, sauce, and casserole, I didn't know there was anything unusual about beginning the day with the scent of olive oil and crushed, fragrant white cloves sautéing in a cast iron pan.

In another country, on another part of the continent, another child was growing up a connoisseur of TV's comedic genre, familiar with the details of each figure's history and risks, and becoming a student of the effort required, and payoff lauded, to make people laugh.

We wouldn't meet until after he had attended a top school for television writing, and I had introduced my whole neighborhood to heavily garlicked pico de gallo and heard from at least one set of (dear) roommates asking me to please limit the house odor of garlic to evening. But when we did meet, it didn't take long for Andy to find out that I had never lived with TV and didn't ever anticipate living with one. And it didn't take long for me to learn that never, not in his parents' home nor his own, had one of the papery white bulbs crossed the threshold. It is fair to say TV and garlic were defining points of both of our rearings by both their presence and absence, certainly in contrast to each other.

And so we came to one of the cruxes of moving forward in our relationship: he would give up TV, and I would give up garlic.

Months later, I was sure there was some subterfuge in the box delivered to our doorstep as a wedding gift—a thirty-two-inch apple of discord. I would not believe that it hadn't been arranged by him to seem like he'd had no hand in it. And if garlic were part of the menu, he wouldn't eat at my parents' and wouldn't kiss me if I had. It was a difficult part of marriage, a time when we were both unsure if what we had lost and given up was worth what we had gained, brokering something deeply meaningful to each of us but repellant to the other, not just culinary and entertainment traditions and habits, because of course, the bulb and tube came to represent so much more than themselves.

It's interesting when we retell this story now, to hear how many people say, "I could never do that," in reference to giving up either one. But fourteen years into voluntary garlic renunciation, at least as its own food group, I've come to desire it both more and less—to appreciate it more, but to be more discriminating about it. When I had it for breakfast every day, the tantalizing smell of garlic in my brother's saffron salad dressing would have been missed. The luxurious richness it gives my father's spaghetti sauce and my mother's cold cucumber soup would have been, not exactly lost, but unnoticed and not appreciated the way I do now. It's made me more sensitive too, if not squeamish about the lingering stink a low-quality Alfredo sauce leaves in the body.

There are many varieties of alliums in our garden—walking onions, beautifully symmetrical round white sweets, and sleek torpedoes; chives; and tall ornamentals, purple balls of poofy exuberance—but no *Allium sativum*. For the record, we never have owned a TV either—the wedding gift was hastily, apologetically returned.

But perhaps we all soften over time, and the inevitability of other screens of all sizes in our lives has made the no-TV rule moot, and seemed, well, inevitable. We've been growing cheery little garlic chives in the garden for the past six years, and if they sometimes make their way into various sauces or soups where they are enjoyed without recognition, well, perhaps that is also inevitable.

Tulips, High and Low

JOHANNA

If the forecast calls for rain on a Tuesday between 4:00 and 8:30 p.m., it can really mess up my neighbor Frans's mowing schedule. His watering schedule is equally strict, but since it's on a timer, his role is merely supervisory. He sits on his front porch every evening in the summer, timing his bedtime by when his sprinklers switch on—the low spray kind, whose degree of spray angle can be adjusted anywhere from 360 to 30 degrees—and then, 15 minutes later, switch off.

Dividing his patch of green from the neighbor's is a juniper hedge, its feather-like branches extending in graceful arcs from the center to the far edge. Frans's side has a perpetual buzzed flattop, a military trim ready to "Yes, sir!" at any moment of any day, any season of the year. In a bed exactly 18 inches deep along the front of his cement porch is a line of miniature red roses, each trimmed the same height (below the porch's bottom railing), the soil around each kept scraped.

Despite immigrating to the United States as a teen in the early 1950s—alone, landing as a farmhand at an egg farm—Frans has held on to his Dutch identity in much the same way that he's hung on to his Dutch accent. He's happy to help change kids' bike tires and show you the aluminum tool he's carried with him since his days as a kid in Rotterdam; he's happy to talk sea dikes and wooden shoes, all the while ribbing that "if you're not Dutch, you're not much." But mention tulips and his teasing, jovial countenance darkens.

There's never been a tulip on Frans's side of the hedge, never so much as a little spike of

Forcing Hyacinth Bulbs

If you live in a place where the end of January leaves you longing for something fresh and bright, mark your calendar for the first and second weeks of December to start some forced hyacinths—six to eight weeks before you need those blooms and that aroma to transport you to spring. Beginning with big, unblemished bulbs, tuck them in a pot of loose-draining, gritty soil, leaving a third of the bulb peeking out. Keep the pot hydrated (but not too wet) and in a cool, dark spot for the first four weeks or so until a couple inches of growth clear the bulb. Then bring them into the warmth and light. In about two weeks, an aromatic burst of spring color will brighten your mood and carry you through till the daylight hours are long enough to assure you that, truly, spring will come again this year.

green leaf between the mini roses in the spring before they've blossomed into a line of red architectural trim.

Bulbs, such as tulips, are unique in the plant world in that a true bulb can hold all of what the plant needs for its entire life cycle in underground storage systems. Alliums, such as onions and garlic, are also true bulbs, but despite tulips being members of the same plant family as onions, there is a reason they have never caught on as a mainstream food source. There was a time in history, though, when a desperate attempt was made to make them so.

The Dutch called it the Hunger Winter, the unusually harsh winter of 1944–45 when Frans was eight years old. While other parts of Europe were being liberated, the northern part of the Netherlands remained under Nazi occupation. There was nothing on store shelves, and if a farmer had food, it had to be traded for; no one would take money. German occupiers were diverting anything they deemed edible to support their own troops. But the nation's seed bulbs were in wintering barns, unplanted from the year before because of the war situation. In desperation, people experimented with preparing the old dried bulbs for eating, learning how to remove the papery exterior and the yellow-green core, as these would make you ill. Nobody liked them, but most people tried them. In order to not get too sick, you couldn't eat too many. They had very little nutritive value, but they filled the belly.

By the winter of 1944-45, Frans and his little brother, like so many other city children, were walking many kilometers out of the city, going from farm to farm begging

Start a Tulip Tradition

Tulip petals are fully edible if they are rinsed of pollen and have never been sprayed. They range in flavor from none at all to slightly beany. If you can bear to disassemble a blossom, toss the petals in a bowl of lettuce leaves for a bright rainbow of springtime salad. Or turn an ordinary hors d'oeuvre dip into pretty canapés: fill each petal with a spoonful of something savory—guacamole, baba ghanoush, herbed goat cheese, et cetera—and arrange in a sunburst on a platter or cake stand.

for food. Eventually, even the farmers had no spare bread to hand out. Frans and his little brother were taught to eat tulip bulbs, a steep fall for the tulip, which had been, in Holland's tulip heyday, more valuable than gold, even used as a kind of currency.

When the war ended, tulips gradually returned to being the commercial crop they had been before; bread and potatoes, cheese, and butter eventually were purchasable again, but not before an estimated eighteen to twenty-two thousand people died that season of slow starvation, and a new parenting refrain, "You're not hungry, you just have an appetite," was embedded in the psyches of the coming generation of children who knew, indeed, what hunger was.

And Frans? Much like a tulip bulb, he seemed to have stored within himself all the life forces necessary to grow and bloom despite the horrors of war and hunger, and the alienation of being an immigrant. Sitting on his front porch in the glowing summer evening sunset, surveying his impeccable $1\frac{3}{4}$-inch lawn and trimmed hedge, but referring to his safe warm home, his car, stocked kitchen, and mostly his life full of caring family and friends, he says, "I'm so lucky. I feel so blessed."

How

The basics are very much the same whether you're propagating daffodils, tulips, hyacinths, Muscari, or even garlic. The actual mechanics of separating bulbs and their little bulblets are very simple.

ONE

Gently lift the clump of bulbs out of the ground with a garden fork after it has finished flowering and the leaves have died back.

TWO

Moving quickly and covering the part you're not working on with wet burlap so the roots don't dry out, gently rock, twist, or pull the big and small bulbs apart from each other.

THREE

Replant them, giving each a few inches space from one another. The small bulbs will take a few years to be big enough to blossom, but the larger ones may produce the following spring, and certainly the spring after that.

Ready for bulb propagation 2.0?

Look up "chipping" for tulip and daffodil bulbs, and "scaling" for lilies. Both of these simple DIY techniques involve dividing the actual bulb, making sure that a part of the hard bottom of the bulb where the roots emerge, the "basal plate," remains on each "chip" or slice. New little bulblets will grow from here, and in about eight to ten weeks, they will be big enough to pot up. This is the quickest way to increase the number of bulbs, but it will still take a couple years for the newly divided bulbs to be up to flowering.

When

Division of bulbs is best done during their dormant season, but because this is when they are invisible from the top of the soil, you will either need to mark where they are while they are blooming, or dig them up to divide them while they still have green leaves. If timing necessitates the latter, wait till the bloom has died back and make sure to keep the leaves intact so they can keep photosynthesizing and feeding the bulb to be ready for next year's growth and blooming.

Why

Bulbs produce flowers faster than seeds from the same plant, and they produce plants that are genetically identical. They are also easier to find and simpler to germinate.

Who

Amaryllis, crocus, daffodil, garlic, gladiolus, hyacinth, lily, Muscari, narcissus, onion, tulip, and more.

Difficulty

Easy.

Glossary

bulb: Built of thick, fleshy layers formed below the soil, a bulb holds all the nutrients necessary for a plant to go through its life cycle. A small bulb growing from the base of another bulb, rather like an underground pup, is called a bulbel.

corm: A short, rounded storage-purposed stem covered with papery leaves, such as the corms of crocuses, cyclamens, and gladiolus. A small corm growing from the base of another corm, rather like an underground pup, is called a cormel.

basal plate: The hard disk the roots grow out of at the bottom of a bulb or a corm.

CAUTIONS

CAUTIONS

JOHANNA

Romance, beauty, delicate aromas, shared memories. These are the emotions of a Paris honeymoon and, we hope, your burgeoning memory garden. But we would be remiss to not share with you a few cautions and cautionary tales as you begin plant propagation in earnest.

Our Paris honeymoon fell into place too easily. We found ridiculously inexpensive airfare and then an even cheaper three-star hotel on Priceline. The ticket agent even upgraded us to first class when she learned it was our *lune de miel*. Love must have still filled our eyes at the ticket counter.

Soon our free drinks and lavish food were interrupted by my post-wedding-day migraine. Vomit bags are vomit bags, first class or coach. Upon arriving at our hotel, we learned discount Internet vacation booking was still in its infancy in 2002. Our three-star hotel attracted two types of clients—American tourists and French workers who sublet and shared their rooms by the hour. We, at least, got free breakfast.

Breakfast was beautiful flaky chocolate croissants and tiny little glass jars of Bonne Maman jam. These last were completely adorable, and to my new husband's great embarrassment, I carefully snuck several into my bag every day to bring home to nieces and nephews who would be enchanted by their tiny size.

We spent our days away from the red-light district, walking the streets of Paris. As my new husband was unwilling to spring for entrance fees, we did a great deal of looking at things from the bottom (*salut*, footings of *la Tour Eiffel*) and outside (*bonjour*, exterior doors of *le Louvre*). I found a hairdresser who cut off my hair—about 20 thick, straight, blond inches of it. Alas, what I saw as a symbol of a willingness to be vulnerable in beginning a new life together felt to my man like some kind of a bait and switch, a reaction that I

134

reacted against, most understandably. My husband did finally agree to enter one museum, the *Musée des Égouts de Paris*, the Paris Sewer Museum.

When our week came to a close, we learned that our daily croissant and pilfered jam had not been free as we thought. Breakfast had cost us fifteen euros daily *each*, nearly doubling the cost of our stay. At this point in the checkout process, furious and unable to express himself in French, my husband spun on his heel, pulling his rolling bag behind, and—now to *my* great embarrassment—in a language that needs no interpretation, spat on the floor. At least I had some little jams to show for it.

I'd also tucked some tiny, fragrant tangerines into my purse to savor at home in the snows of December. And there they stayed all the way across the Atlantic Ocean until my husband turned me over to the customs officer in the airport, who, no, wouldn't even let me quickly rip off the skin and stuff the juicy little ball into my mouth before I stepped through the security check.

Marriages and gardens sometimes begin kind of ugly. I have since learned there are steps you can take with both to help them be successful and beautiful.

Laws

For starters, in fact there *are* laws about bringing plant material, including fresh fruit, across international borders. Stop here if you'd rather ask forgiveness.

United States law requires that every fruit and vegetable be declared to a customs or border patrol officer and be presented for inspection. Entry requirements for other plant material that will be used for growing varies by plant, but all plants must meet certain requirements. You'll need a permit for twelve or more; plants must have a phytosanitary certificate from the country of origin; they have to be bare rooted with no growing media attached to the roots; and they should have no bugs or sickly looking plant parts. Border Patrol agents are not life-form discriminators; just as with humans, if the plants do not meet entry requirements, they will be refused entry.

Soil-Borne Diseases

Most of your plant propagation will likely happen in one country, and to prepare for that, you should know a bit about soil ecology.

Healthy soil is just exuberant with microscopic life, and part of that life always includes organisms that grow by consuming the same things we want to consume (even if our consumption of them is just with our eyes or nose). Those organisms that weaken and kill the things they feed off of, we categorize as pathogens or, more to the point, pests.

Microscopic pests fall into these categories: fungi, nematodes, bacteria, and viruses. Most soil-borne diseases are caused by the first two, but the others are around too. When sharing plants and the soil they are rooted in, you should know that it is possible for something truly pestiferous to piggyback with the gift.

The good news is, just like in our own bodies, although undesirable organisms in soil may always be present, they are kept in check from harming the plants or colonizing the soil by all the good organisms present. In fact, the best ways to combat soil disease are to add compost—the deeply composted black-gold type—and practice good garden hygiene. Remove any infected plant material as soon as you spot it, and always wash your tools after using them on plants you suspect are infected. If you're concerned about your tools rusting, give them a wash with rubbing alcohol, which will quickly evaporate. Do not compost any infected plant material; it should be thrown away. Keep plants spaced so that air can circulate around them. This will minimize conditions that favor fungal diseases.

Stowaways: Bugs and Seeds

Not all pests are microscopic of course. Leaves, stems, seeds, and dead plant material are all places that unwanted insects or their eggs could be hidden, so do a thorough inspection and brush or pick off anything suspicious before you bring it home.

If you're bringing home shared soil, it could also be harboring stowaway seeds for a plant you're not as interested in propagating. The way to prevent unwanted seeds from colonizing your garden is to quarantine your plant. Rather than putting it directly in your soil among your other plants, give it a while inside or in a separated spot, like a patio, to grow out any unwanted seeds and see if it, by chance, is infected.

Invaders and Crusaders

Be careful if you don't know what a plant is or what its growth and reproductive habits are. Unidentified species can also be invasive species. You don't want to introduce something into your garden (and neighborhood) hoping it will bring happy memories, only to find what it has actually gifted you with is hours of frustrating weed removal. If you're bringing the plant from a different kind of environment where it seemed to grow in a restrained and pleasing manner, it is still possible that in *your* environment it could go wild.

Ethical Decisions

Finally, there is the question of when is it right and when is it dishonorable to take plant material for propagating. If it's a family member you're collecting from, they'll likely be delighted you care, that they are connected in your good memories. In public settings, or on other private property, a good rule of thumb is to ask first before you go snipping, clipping, and seed swiping. If that's not practical or reasonable, you get to come up with your own code of what is right. For instance, I feel comfortable taking plant material from public places if I know it is going to be pruned or thrown away anyway. I have been known to help myself to seeds from plants on the public property side of a private property fence, but only if it looks like the seeds are going to end up fallen and forgotten.

I'd like to think I follow philosopher Immanuel Kant's idea of an unconditional and binding moral law, where the rightness of an act is determined by whether you could consistently let everyone do the same, but then I have moments like that evening walk at Monticello, in Virginia. Monticello had been on my travel bucket list, but by the time my kids and I had driven out of DC and through the misty rolling hills of rural Virginia, I had missed the garden tour. The docents graciously let us walk the half mile back to the parking lot from the house tour unattended, and heaven help me if I didn't pause to help myself to some of the surrounding woods—practically parking lot, really. I slid a few little tubers of dwarf iris, not yet bloomed, into the bag I keep in my purse for unexpected changes of pants (my three-year-old), and then into my dear friend's fridge until I could fly back home across the country. Was I right to do it? In case not, we picked up all the litter we could find along the way as a kind of sorry-not-sorry apology.

You'll figure out what feels right for you when it comes to collecting plant material, but one thing I know for certain, when it comes to small fragrant citrus or a bit of root from a historic landmark, I'm more likely to ask forgiveness than permission. Hopefully I could just offer a plant start I've propagated as a peace offering instead of either.

RESOURCES

Introduction

Where to buy wintergreen: **ediblelandscaping.com.**

Wintergreen grows in acidic soil. Shelle Wells of **preparednessmama.com** gives directions for two free ways to do a pH test on your soil using common household ingredients: **preparednessmama.com/ testing-your-soil-ph-without-a-kit/.**

Water Rooting

A rainbow of coleus plants can be found at **taylorgreenhouses.com** and at **rosydawngardens.com.**

A great many herb plants can be found at **thegrowers-exchange.com,** and **richters. com** carries a wide variety of herb seeds.

Stem Cuttings

For willows of many varieties:

In USA: Vermont Willow Nursery, **willowsvermont.com.**

In Canada: Lakeshore Willows, **lakeshorewillows.com.**

For fig trees, look through the offerings at Four Winds Growers, **fourwindsgrowers. com,** and Raintree Nursery, **raintreenursery.com.**

Planting Pups

To learn more, or obtain bromeliads, start with **bromeliads.info.**

This site includes five places to buy bromeliads. You can also often find them at local grocery stores in the floral section.

Where to get birdcage decorations:

HobbyLobby.com and **Save-on-crafts.com** carry them new; try **Craigslist.org** or wedding recycling sites, such as **Ruffledblog.com/recycle-your-wedding** for a deal on secondhand ones.

Where to buy sempervivum plants in bulk: **Mountaincrestgardens.com** and **simplysucculents.com.**

Some sources for fun interview questions:

Table Topics makes whole boxes of interesting questions, themed to different groups: **tabletopics.com.**

You can also find great question lists at the following websites:

schmidtgen.com/wordpress/2014/10/01/ 100-questions-about-your-childhood/; legacyproject.org/guides/lifeintquestions. pdf; storycorps.org/great-questions/.

Old fashioned lollipops on sticks: Startup's Candy Company, **startupcandy.com.**

You can buy wool felt at The Felt Pod, **thefeltpod.com.**

Knit Picks, an extensive yarn and fiber store, carries dye in 27 colors to dye the wool: **knitpicks.com.**

Leaf Cuttings

Amazon, eBay, and Etsy may not be where you first think to look for hard-to-find plants, but, amazingly, you can find many plants for sale at these big Internet sites, including jade trees and African violets. Grocery stores and home improvement stores sometimes stock them seasonally.

The Violet Barn (**violetbarn.com**) carries hundreds of kinds of African violets, collected from all over the world, many rare or unusual.

Commercial plant propagating trays, which usually include a heat source to warm the soil from beneath, can be found at most big-box hardware and garden stores. You can buy a heat mat to stick under propagating trays you have created yourself from the same places. More decorative propagators, which work like a terrarium in keeping moisture in around the plant and can be searched online with the words "closed terrarium," can be found at Gardenista (**gardenista.com**) for expensive ones, and IKEA (**ikea.com**) for cheaper ones shaped like little houses.

Layering

Scotch broom and Japanese honeysuckle are considered invasive species, so if you choose to grow them, please keep them under control. You can read more about them at **thewildclassroom.com**. Poison ivy also invades, but is not listed because it is native to North America.

High Country Roses (**highcountryroses. com**) sells Austrian copper, or Austrian briar roses.

You can find a seek-no-further apple tree at Trees of Antiquity, **treesofantiquity.com**.

Crown Division

Michael Lang, of Green Mountain Hosta Nursery, is putting honeybells hostas into his next catalog just for us! He says it is the most fragrant hosta, and it is more vigorous than the other fragrant hostas. Thank you, Michael. (**greenmountainhosta.com**)

You can buy sand, portland cement, and sheets of plastic at your local building supply store.

Root Division

Horseradish root sources:

Nourse Farms Small Fruit Nursery (**noursefarms.com**) sells horseradish roots of the "big top" strain because they have found those plants to grow well in a wide range of hardiness zones.

Jung Garden and Flower Seed Company (**jungseed.com**) sells the variety bohemian horseradish crowns and sets, and says the added bonus of planting horseradish as a companion planting is that the leaves are a trap crop for flea beetles.

Saving Cucurbit Seeds

For many interesting and beautiful varieties of cucurbit seeds, visit Sustainable Seed

Company (**sustainableseedco.com**) and Baker Creek Heirloom Seeds (**rareseeds. com**).

A wildly beautiful book about melons: *Melons for the Passionate Grower* by Amy Goldman.

An accessible and engaging book on plant breeding in your own garden: *Plant Breeding for the Home Gardener* by Joseph Tychonievich.

Simple Seed Saving

An excellent resource on all things seed saving: **seedsavers.org**.

For ink-making supplies (which can sometimes also be found at Michaels, and even Walmart):

Gum arabic: **bulkapothecary.com**;
Soda ash: **dickblick.com**;
Calligraphy nibs: **dickblick.com**.

A gallery of beautiful seed photographs are found in this book: *Seeing Seeds: A Journey into the World of Seedheads, Pods, and Fruit* by Teri Dunn Chase and Robert Llewellyn.

Ashworth, Suzanne, and Kent Whealy. *Seed to Seed: Seed Saving and Growing Techniques for Vegetable Gardeners*. Decorah, IA: Seed Savers Exchange, 2002. (The definitive reference for home gardeners seeking to save their own seeds.)

Bulbs and Corms

Sources for bulbs and corms:

John Scheepers Bulbs, **johnscheepers.com**.

Van Engelen Inc. (**vanengelen.com**), the partner company of John Scheepers, sells bulbs in bulk for wholesale prices.

Brent and Becky's Bulbs, **brentandbeckysbulbs.com**.

Dutch Gardens, **dutchgardens.com**.

Further Inspiration

Walden at West Bloomfield—Creating a Literary Garden, **waldenatwestbloomfield.blogspot. com**.

Druse, Ken. *Making More Plants: The Science, Art, and Joy of Propagation.* Stewart, Tabori, and Chang, 2012.

Stony Hill Gardens' Master Gardener, Carol Bright Stober, is willing to help with plant or insect identification, and other gardening topics. The business is in Chester, New Jersey, so she is most familiar with flora and fauna of Eastern USA. Stony Hill Gardens, (908) 879-2696.

Templates

Templates for folding a paper crane, a felt dove garland, and a seed packet can be found on pages 142, 143, and 144, or as printables at **ellensheppardbuchert.com**.

Folding a Paper Crane Template

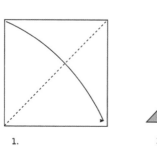

1.

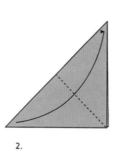

2.

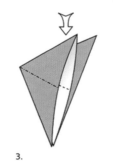

3.

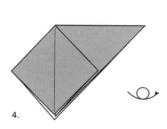

4.

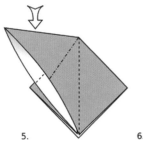

5.

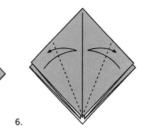

6.

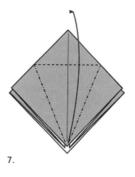

7.

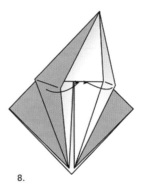

8.

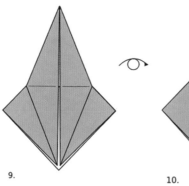

9.

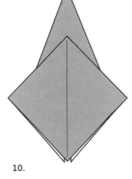

10.

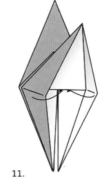

11.

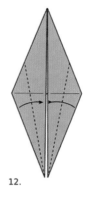

12.

13.

14.

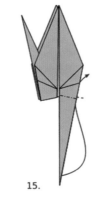

15.

16.

17.

Traditional Japanese Model
Diagram by Andrew Hudson

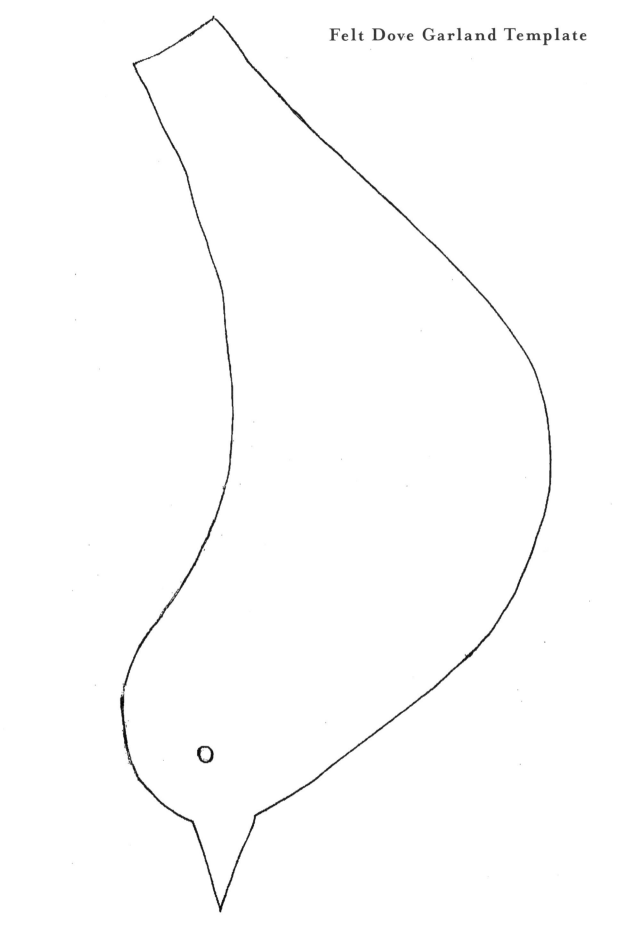

Felt Dove Garland Template

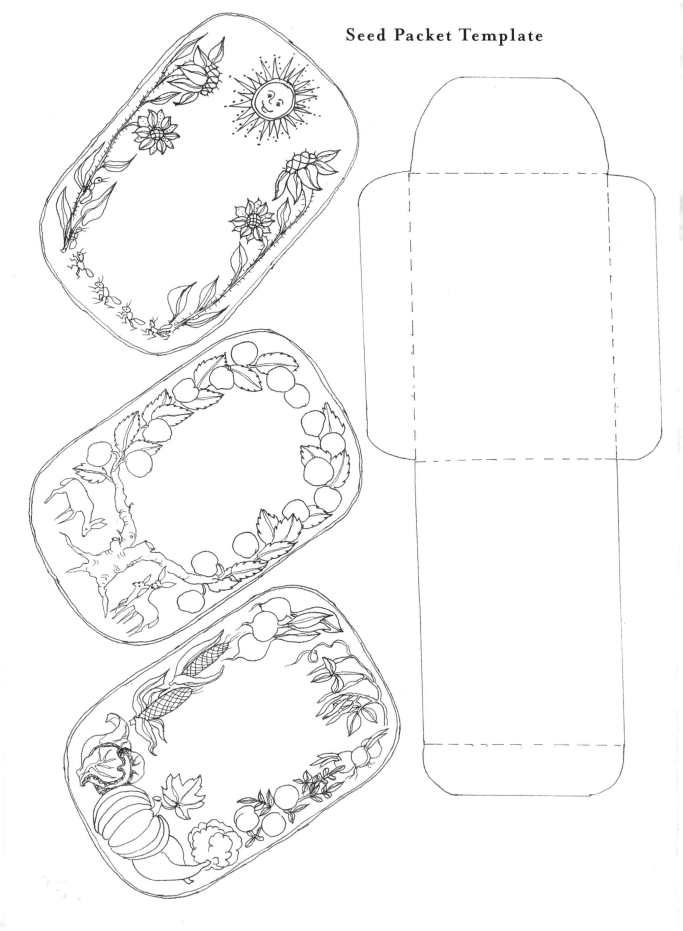

Seed Packet Template